Make:

JUMPSTARTING
the Raspberry Pi
Zero W

CONTROL THE WORLD AROUND
YOU WITH A $10 COMPUTER

Akkana Peck

MAKER MEDIA
SAN FRANCISCO, CA

Published by Maker Media, Inc., 1700 Montgomery Street, Suite 240, San Francisco, CA 94111

Maker Media books may be purchased for educational, business, or sales promotional use. Online editions are also available for most titles (*safaribooksonline.com*). For more information, contact our corporate/institutional sales department: 800-998-9938 or *corporate@oreilly.com*.

Publisher: Roger Stewart
Editor: Patrick DiJusto
Copy Editor: Elizabeth Welch, Happenstance Type-O-Rama
Proofreader: Scout Festa, Happenstance Type-O-Rama
Interior Designer and Compositor: Maureen Forys, Happenstance Type-O-Rama
Cover Designer: Maureen Forys, Happenstance Type-O-Rama
Indexer: Valerie Perry, Happenstance Type-O-Rama

All the circuit and component diagrams in this book are created using Fritzing (*http://fritzing.org/home*).

August 2017: First Edition

Revision History for the First Edition
2017-08-28 First Release

See *oreilly.com/catalog/errata.csp?isbn=9781680454567* for release details.

978-1-680-45-456-7

Safari® Books Online

Safari Books Online is an on-demand digital library that delivers expert content in both book and video form from the world's leading authors in technology and business. Technology professionals, software developers, web designers, and business and creative professionals use Safari Books Online as their primary resource for research, problem solving, learning, and certification training. Safari Books Online offers a range of plans and pricing for enterprise, government, education, and individuals. Members have access to thousands of books, training videos, and prepublication manuscripts in one fully searchable database from publishers like O'Reilly Media, Prentice Hall Professional, Addison-Wesley Professional, Microsoft Press, Sams, Que, Peachpit Press, Focal Press, Cisco Press, John Wiley & Sons, Syngress, Morgan Kaufmann, IBM Redbooks, Packt, Adobe Press, FT Press, Apress, Manning, New Riders, McGraw-Hill, Jones & Bartlett, Course Technology, and hundreds more. For more information about Safari Books Online, please visit us online.

How to Contact Us

Please address comments and questions to the publisher:

Maker Media
1700 Montgomery St.
Suite 240
San Francisco, CA 94111

You can send comments and questions to us by email at *books@makermedia.com*.

Maker Media unites, inspires, informs, and entertains a growing community of resourceful people who undertake amazing projects in their backyards, basements, and garages. Maker Media celebrates your right to tweak, hack, and bend any Technology to your will. The Maker Media audience continues to be a growing culture and community that believes in bettering ourselves, our environment, our educational system—our entire world. This is much more than an audience, it's a worldwide movement that Maker Media is leading. We call it the Maker Movement.

To learn more about Make: visit us at *makezine.com*. You can learn more about the company at the following websites:

Maker Media: *makermedia.com*

Maker Faire: *makerfaire.com*

Maker Shed: *makershed.com*

DEDICATION

To Dave: husband, friend, life companion...plus editor and proofreader

CONTENTS

ACKNOWLEDGMENTS

Any book represents the work of a team, not just a single author.

I'd like to thank my husband Dave for his endless work reviewing each draft and helping rein in my prolixity—not to mention putting up with my angst and bellyaching when things didn't work as expected.

The staff at Maker Media—Liz, Maureen, and especially my editor, Patrick—were ever helpful and patient, putting up with my constant stream of rewrites and trying to work through the various software problems we encountered.

And let's not forget all the folks who share open source code and libraries. Without them, the Pi Zero W would never light a single LED.

The wiring diagrams in the book were made with Fritzing, a terrific free tool for sharing circuit information (*http://fritzing.org/*). The images were edited with GIMP, the premiere open source image editing tool. The Fritzing .fzz and GIMP .xcf files are on the book's GitHub repository, *https://github.com/akkana/pi-zero-w-book*.

1

Getting Started

Why choose the Raspberry Pi Zero W? It's small. It's cheap. It's power efficient. It has WiFi and Bluetooth Low Energy (BLE) built in. And it has the same general-purpose input/output (GPIO) header that bigger Raspberry Pis have: the gateway to controlling all sorts of hardware.

It's easy to build gizmos that use hardware and networking in fun ways. In this book, you'll build three projects using the Pi Zero W:

* Blinking LEDs

* An environmental monitor that can keep track of the temperature in your house, and even turn on your fan or air conditioner before you get home from work

* A wearable light string that monitors news feeds and websites to alert you when there's something interesting going on

You don't need much prior experience with either hardware or programming—though knowing how to solder will help.

With what you learn from these projects, you can extend the Pi's power to hundreds of other hardware and software projects.

HARDWARE REQUIREMENTS

Each chapter opens with a list of hardware required to finish the project. That makes it easy to know you have what you need without running to the electronics store every half hour, or if you live in a remote area, waiting several days for mail order.

Here's the hardware you'll need for this introductory chapter:

* The Raspberry Pi Zero W itself (though you can follow along on any Raspberry Pi)

* A power source: 5 volts, at least 1 amp, with a MicroUSB plug

* A microSD card, preferably at least 8 GB, to use with a monitor (you can get by with 4 GB if you only want to run "headless")

* Another computer with WiFi and a MicroSD writer

To use the PIXEL desktop, you'll need the following:

* A monitor, keyboard, and mouse

* A cable that connects mini-HDMI to your monitor

* A USB hub, ideally one with external power and not USB 3: either a hub that plugs into MicroUSB, or a regular hub plus a USB On-the-Go (OTG) adapter

Now let's look at the board itself.

ABOUT THE RASPBERRY PI ZERO W

The technical specs of the Pi Zero W are as follows:

* 1 GHz, single-core ARM11 Broadcom CPU

* 512 MB of RAM

* MicroSD card slot

* MicroUSB power connector

* Mini-HDMI video port

* MicroUSB On-the-Go (OTG) port

* Hardware Attached on Top (HAT)-compatible 40-pin header

* Composite video and reset headers

* CSI camera connector

* 802.11n wireless LAN

* Bluetooth Low Energy 4.0

FIGURE 1.1: The small but mighty Raspberry Pi Zero W

The Pi Zero W sports a fairly punchy processor for such a small, inexpensive device—not as hot as the larger Pi 3, but faster than the original Raspberry Pi—and it can run a full version of Linux. That means you have hundreds of programs and libraries already available, and you can write your own software for it in any language of your choice. Most examples in this book will use Python: it's the most flexible, the easiest to learn, and very well supported.

The Pi Zero W doesn't arrive with an operating system, or even any built-in storage. It has to boot from a MicroSD card with an OS installed.

The most popular OS for the Raspberry Pi family is Raspbian, a version of Debian Linux. It's built for the ARM CPU and customized for the Raspberry Pi, so that's what you'll use with this book. You can also run other versions of Linux, such as Arch or Gentoo, as well as specialized distributions optimized for tasks like playing video on your TV. But the Zero W isn't the best choice for such heavy lifting; for TV you're better off choosing the faster Raspberry Pi 3.

You can buy MicroSD cards that already have Raspbian installed, but it's easy to download and install yourself. You'll need a computer (not the Pi itself) that can write to an SD card.

INSTALLING RASPBIAN

Since you can't boot your Pi Zero W until you install an OS to the SD card, you'll do this step with your existing computer.

You can download Raspbian from the Raspberry Pi Foundation: *https://www.raspberrypi.org/downloads/raspbian/*

It gives you two options: install just Raspbian, or install something called NOOBS (which stands for New Out Of the Box Software). NOOBS gives you links to install several different OS options, including Raspbian, but it's a larger download and takes longer to install. For this book, choose Raspbian.

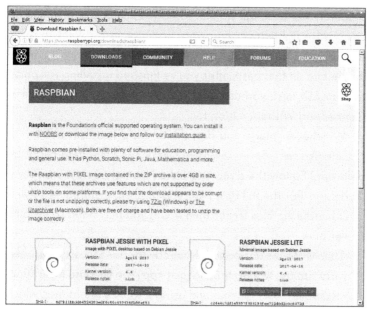

FIGURE 1.2: The Raspbian download page

On the Raspbian download page, you'll see two options:

* Raspbian Jessie with PIXEL

* Raspbian Jessie Lite

Raspbian is a version of Debian, and Debian versions are named after characters from the *Toy Story* movies. Raspbian is currently based on the last version of Debian, named Jessie—the Yodeling Cowgirl from *Toy Story 2* and 3. As this book was being written, Debian released a newer version, named Stretch, after a stretchy purple octopus from *Toy Story 3*. Raspbian will eventually upgrade to Stretch, but there shouldn't be much difference on the surface.

PIXEL is the name of the desktop Raspbian uses—the interface and menus you see on the screen when you connect a monitor to the Pi. If you plan to connect your Pi to a monitor, you definitely want the full version with PIXEL. If you're planning on using it for lightweight hardware projects, never want to run a desktop, and want to save space on the SD card, you can choose Jessie Lite. In that case, after you've finished installing Raspbian to your SD card, you can skip ahead to the section "Headless: Connecting Without a Monitor."

Whichever image you download, unzip it to get a file with a name like `2017-04-10-raspbian-jessie.img`. (The date might be different.) Follow the directions linked from the Raspbian Download page. For the full Raspbian, if your unzip program is old and can't handle zip files larger than 4 GB, you may need to install a newer one.

Then write the unzipped file directly to your SD card. You need to overwrite the whole card, not just copy the file onto a partition. The Raspbian folks recommend using a tool called Etcher, which you can find at *https://etcher.io/*. But they also have instructions for people who want more control over the process: Windows users can use Win32DiskImager, and Mac and Linux people can use dd. If you're a Chromebook user, Raspbian doesn't have a page for you, but if you use developer mode and bring up a terminal, you can follow the dd instructions meant for Linux users.

CONNECTING TO A MONITOR, KEYBOARD, AND MOUSE

You now have Raspbian installed and you're ready to try it. If you don't have a monitor handy and want to run headless, skip ahead to the section "Headless: Connecting Without a Monitor."

The Pi Zero W has a built-in mini-HDMI video port. So you will need a cable that connects from mini-HDMI to whatever your monitor requires, like HDMI or DVI, or you'll have to use adapters on a regular HDMI cable.

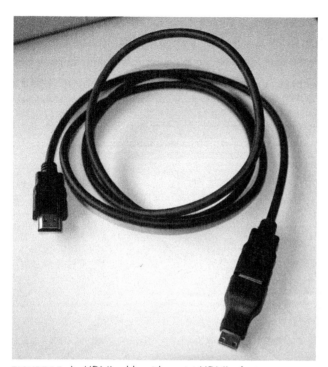

FIGURE 1.3: An HDMI cable with a mini-HDMI adapter

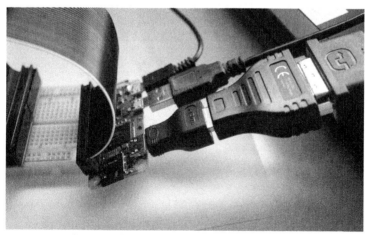

FIGURE 1.4: Adapters galore! A video adapter from mini-HDMI to regular HDMI, and then to DVI, plus a USB OTG adapter. The Pi Zero W also has a ribbon cable attached to it.

You'll also need a USB hub. The Pi Zero W has only a single MicroUSB port (plus a power port that uses the same connector), but you'll need a place to plug in both a keyboard and a mouse. The hub can be a little tricky: Pis have known problems connecting to some cheap unpowered hubs and trouble driving slow hardware like a mouse or keyboard off a USB 3 hub. Your best bet is a USB 2 hub with an external power supply.

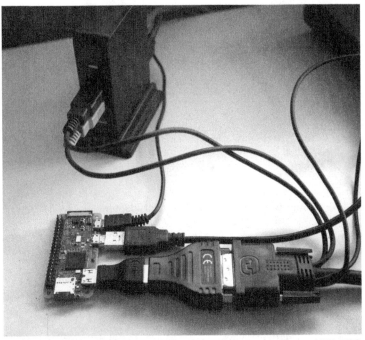

FIGURE 1.5: The powered USB 2 hub is plugged in to the Pi via a USB OTG adapter. The author's DVI KVM is connected via two adapters to the Zero W's mini HDMI, and the mouse and keyboard cables from the KVM plug into the USB hub. Whew!

You might also need a special USB cable. Most hubs have a regular USB A plug. But you need a hub specifically intended for computers with MicroUSB, or an adapter that goes from MicroUSB to your hub. One option is a MicroUSB-to-USB A female adapter, sometimes called a USB OTG adapter; they're inexpensive and will probably be useful for a variety of purposes on the Pi Zero W.

FIGURE 1.6: A USB On-the-Go (OTG) adapter

Got your mini-HDMI and USB hub all set up? It's time to try booting the Pi Zero W with a monitor. Skip ahead to "Logging In and Changing the Default Password."

HEADLESS: CONNECTING WITHOUT A MONITOR

The Raspberry Pi Zero W is a great hardware controller. It's small and power efficient, and it has all those hardware outputs. You might have bought it purely for that purpose and have no intention of connecting it to a monitor.

But how do you get your software on it or test it?

Fortunately, there are several ways to connect over the Pi Zero W's built-in WiFi. The easiest is Secure Shell, or SSH. But before you can do that, you have to set up wireless on the SD card so that the Pi will boot and automatically connect itself to the network.

Start by plugging your Raspbian SD card into your computer. If you've just finished copying Raspbian to the card, eject the card and reinsert it to force the computer to read and mount the new partitions you just wrote onto the card.

Normal Raspbian (not NOOBS) uses two partitions on the SD card. The first is the boot partition: it contains a Linux kernel and some startup files like drivers for hardware the Pi can't do without. The second is the root partition, where most of Raspbian's files are. The root partition is formatted as the native Linux ext4 filesystem, and you probably won't be able to mount it except from another Linux computer. Fortunately, you can do the configuration you're most likely to need using only the boot partition, which you can mount on any computer. Mount that partition now.

Configuring SSH and WiFi from Another Computer

Raspbian has SSH out of the box, but it's disabled by default. To enable it, create a file called `ssh` on the SD card's boot partition. The file can be empty; all that matters is that it's named `ssh`. Now Raspbian will start SSH the next time you boot.

That's the easy part. Next you have to set up the Pi's network connection.

If your WiFi network uses Dynamic Host Configuration Protocol, or DHCP (which handles automatic addressing), and doesn't have a password or any browser authentication screens, the Pi should connect on its own. In that case, skip ahead to "Finding Your Pi on the Local Network." Otherwise, you can configure networking by creating a file on the boot partition called `wpa_supplicant.conf`.

You'll need the name of your network, called the service set identifier (SSID). That's what you normally see in your computer's menus when you connect. Of course, you'll need your network password if you have one.

If your network requires browser authentication—in other words, if you connect to the network without a password, then go to a web page where you type in a password—you're probably out of luck. There's no easy way to set up a computer to do that automatically. If plugging in a monitor isn't possible, you have a couple more options. You can use a USB Ethernet dongle with an OTG adapter. Or you can buy a USB serial cable made for a Raspberry Pi, in which case you'll need to edit `config.txt` on the SD card's boot partition and add these two lines to enable a serial console and disable Bluetooth:

```
enable_uart=1
dtoverlay=pi3-disable-bt
```

But back to configuring WiFi.

Got your SSID and password ready? Create `wpa_supplicant.conf` by opening it with whatever text editor you prefer. You must use a plain text editor, not a word processor like Word. If you don't already have a text editor you use regularly, try Notepad on Windows, TextEdit on Mac, or nano on Linux.

Enter this:

```
ctrl_interface=DIR=/var/run/wpa_supplicant GROUP=netdev
update_config=1

country=US
network={
    ssid="YOUR SSID"
    psk="YOUR PASSWORD"
}
```

in which YOUR SSID is replaced by the SSID of your network, and YOUR PASSWORD is replaced by your network password. If your network doesn't have a password, use this instead:

```
network={
    ssid="YOUR SSID"
    key_mgmt=NONE
}
```

If your SSID is hidden (it doesn't show up automatically when you scan for networks), it might help to add this line after the `key_mgmt` line:

```
scan_ssid=1
```

Save the file and exit.

To use a static IP address, rather than one dynamically configured with DHCP, you need an extra step. (If you aren't sure, you probably won't need this step.)

You'll need to mount the Raspbian partition, the second partition on the hard drive. It's an ext4 format filesystem, so you'll probably need access to a Linux machine for this part. In `etc` on the Raspbian partition, edit the file `dhcpcd.conf`. Add a section at the bottom with your static network information:

```
interface wlan0
static ip_address=192.168.1.x
static routers=192.168.1.1
static domain_name_servers=192.168.1.1
```

Replace `192.168.1.x` and, if needed, the other addresses with the ones for your network. Save the file and exit. You're ready to try booting.

FINDING YOUR PI ON THE LOCAL NETWORK

If you're connecting to your Pi over the network rather than using a monitor and you're not using a static IP address, you'll have to figure out what address it ended up using. That will be four numbers separated by dots, like 192.168.1.125.

If you're on your own home network and you can log in to your WiFi router (usually by using a browser to navigate to *http://192.168.1.1*), there's probably a Devices tab that shows all devices currently on the network. Look for a new or unfamiliar device: that's probably your Pi. It might even show a hostname of *raspberrypi*.

If you do a web search, you'll find utilities to search for Raspberry Pis on the local network, like the Adafruit-Pi-Finder. But here are some lower-level ways to search for your Pi.

Using *arp* and *fping*

If you can install the `fping` program, here's a fast way to find Raspberry Pis on your network:

```
fping -a -r1 -g 192.168.1.0/24  &> /dev/null
arp -n | fgrep " b8:27:eb"
```

Raspberry Pi WiFi chips have Ethernet addresses that start with `b8:27:eb`, so this looks only for Raspberry Pis on the network.

If you can't install `fping`, try the `arp` command anyway. It might not see a newly booted Pi, but it's worth a try.

If it doesn't find anything, a more reliable program is `nmap`.

Using *nmap*

You can find all the machines on your local network with the command `nmap`. Linux machines probably have `nmap` already, but on a Mac or Windows machine you can get it from *https://nmap.org/download.html*. If your network is 192.168.1:

```
sudo nmap -sn 192.168.1.0/24
```

You can search for only Raspberry Pi devices this way:

```
$ sudo nmap -sn 192.168.1.0/24 | grep -i -B 2 B8:27:EB
```

SSHING TO YOUR RASPBERRY PI

Once your Pi is up and running, and you know its network address, you can log in using SSH. On Mac and Linux, and Chromebooks with developer mode, get a terminal and type

Windows doesn't have SSH installed by default, but there are plenty of good SSH programs available. The most popular is a graphical program called PuTTY. You can download graphical SSH programs for Mac and Chrome OS, too.

SSH even lets you run desktop programs on your Pi, using a technique called X forwarding. That requires an X server program on your local computer. Linux comes with X already; on Mac you can download X11 from Apple; on Windows there are various X servers available, such as Xming.

Once you're running X on your local computer, log in to your Pi with ssh -X (that's a capital X) from Mac or Linux, or in PuTTY, enable Connection > SSH > X11 in the PuTTY configuration. Then you can run graphical programs from that shell and they will display on your local machine.

LOGGING IN AND CHANGING THE DEFAULT PASSWORD

You've booted your Pi Zero W and you're ready to log in, whether it's in PIXEL or over SSH. The first time you log in, use the username **pi**, and the password **raspberry**.

If you've enabled SSH, you will see a warning:

```
SSH is enabled and the default password for the 'pi' user has not
been changed.
This is a security risk - please login as the 'pi' user and type
'passwd' to set a new password.
```

You should change the default password!

You can change the password right now using the command line. Bring up a terminal by clicking on the terminal icon at the top of the screen, as shown in Figure 1.7, or by choosing Accessories > Terminal.

FIGURE 1.7: The PIXEL desktop showing a terminal

You'll be working a lot more with the terminal and the command line in later chapters, but for now, just type **passwd** at the prompt:

```
$ passwd
Changing password for pi.
(current) UNIX password:
```

Type the current password, **raspberry**. Then, when prompted, enter your new password.

BASIC CONFIGURATION

The raspi-config program can do a lot of basic configuration. In the terminal, type

```
sudo raspi-config
```

Navigate around this screen by using the up and down arrow keys. Hit Enter to choose one of the categories or to choose an option.

You can change the password (if you didn't already do so from the command line) or set a hostname.

Under Boot Options, you can choose whether to start in the graphical desktop, or skip it and just boot into the command-line interface (CLI) if you're running headless. For each option, you have a choice of whether the user pi will be logged in automatically, or whether you'll have to log in with a password. If you're connecting over the network with SSH, that setting doesn't matter much; you'll have to log in no matter what (though there are ways of using SSH without a password).

Under Localisation Options, you can use Change Locale to change the language and country you use. For instance, if you're in the United States I recommend changing your locale to en_US.UTF-8. The default is en_GB.UTF-8.

When you're finished with Change Locale, press the Tab key. The highlight will jump to Ok and you can press Enter to accept the new locale(s). Next you'll be taken to a screen where you configure the system locale. People in the United States should choose en_US.UTF-8.

The Interfacing Options section lets you enable hardware such as a Pi Camera, if you have one; enable services like SSH or virtual network computing (VNC); or enable hardware options like SPI or I2C (more about those in Chapter 3) Serial, 1-Wire, or Remote GPIO.

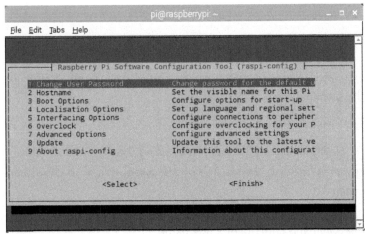

FIGURE 1.8: raspi-config, running in the PIXEL desktop

If you're running a headless Pi, be sure to enable SSH here. The trick of creating a file named ssh on the boot partition works only once. You don't want to have to do that every time you use your Pi!

There are other sections, like Overclocking and Advanced Options, but you shouldn't need to adjust those options.

When you're done configuring, press Tab to get to Finish. raspi-config will prompt you to reboot if you've changed any settings that require a reboot.

THE PIXEL DESKTOP

The Raspberry Pi desktop is called PIXEL. Clicking the raspberry icon in the top left opens a set of menus you can explore. Next to that are icons for a web browser, file manager, and terminal (you'll be using the terminal for most of this book).

The final two icons on the top bar are Wolfram and Mathematica. Wolfram Research made these tools available to Raspberry Pi users free of charge, though you'll probably find them frustratingly slow on the Pi Zero W. If you want to explore the Wolfram world, you're better off with a Raspberry Pi 3.

At the upper right is a networking icon, showing whether your Pi W is connected to WiFi. If you didn't already configure WiFi, you can do it now—the easy way. Click on the WiFi icon in the upper right, choose your network, and set your password.

FIGURE 1.9: Configuring WiFi in PIXEL

Exploring PIXEL

Once WiFi is working, doodle to your heart's content. There are lots of other interesting options under Preferences: you can customize the fonts and colors and the background image, change the behavior of the mouse and keyboard, and add new items to the menu.

You can also install new software. Click the raspberry icon, go to Preferences, and look for Add/Remove Software. There are hundreds of packages you can install, organized by category. You'll install a few of those packages in later chapters.

INTRODUCING THE LINUX COMMAND LINE

A lot of programming requires the command line, so you'll be using the terminal and typing commands a lot with this book. (It's also handy when you're running without a monitor, or debugging something on a device that's at the other side of the house or out in the back yard.)

The program that reads your commands and executes them is called the shell. You'll be using a shell called Bash, short for the Bourne-Again Shell. The name is a pun: the original Unix shell was written by someone named Bourne, but it wasn't open source and couldn't be used in free operating systems like Linux, so the new shell rewritten to replace the Bourne shell was dubbed "Bourne Again."

The first word you type at the shell prompt is a command, and all the words after the command are called arguments. If you want to see the contents of the current directory, type `ls` (a command, short for "list" the contents of the directory). If you want to see the contents of the directory called `python_games`, type `ls python_games`. `ls` is still the command, and `python_games` is the argument.

Some commands require "root privilege," which is like the Administrator account on Windows. For those, you can type **sudo** before the command (sudo is short for Super User DO—in other words, do this command as the super user). Earlier in this chapter you typed **sudo raspi-config** to reconfigure the system.

> **WARNING** Typing commands with sudo **can remove files, remove software, or otherwise damage the Raspbian install. Don't use** sudo **unless you're doing something that really needs it.**

Editing Command Lines

The normal Backspace, Delete, arrow keys, Home, and End work when you're editing commands. But there are some other nice features too.

One example is autocomplete. You hardly ever have to type a whole command; you can hit the Tab key to see what options you have. For instance, typing **ls py** and pressing Tab completes to ls python_games/. (The slash at the end indicates that python_games is a directory, which is the same thing as a folder: it isn't a file; it contains files.)

If there's more than one match, Tab will only complete as far as it can. Typing **ras** and pressing Tab completes to raspi because there are a bunch of different commands that start with raspi. But if you keep hitting Tab (two more times), it will show you the list of everything that matches:

```
pi@raspberrypi:~ $ raspi
raspi-config  raspistill    raspividyuv
raspi-gpio    raspivid      raspiyuv
pi@raspberrypi:~ $ raspi
```

At this point, if you type **-c**, the command will expand to `raspi-config`; if you type **v** instead, it will expand to `raspivid`, which would let you take videos with a camera module if you have one installed.

Some other useful editing shortcuts:

* The up arrow shows you the previous command you typed, which you can edit or change.

* Ctrl-W deletes the last word.

* Ctrl-U deletes back to the beginning of the line.

* Ctrl-K deletes to the end of the line.

* Ctrl-A goes to the beginning of the line, Ctrl-E to the end, Ctrl-B moves backward, Ctrl-F moves forward, Ctrl-H deletes the previous character, and Ctrl-D deletes the next character. These do the same thing as Home, End, Left, Right, Backspace, and Delete, but you can type them without moving your hands from the normal typing position.

* If you need to page up to see earlier commands you typed, use Shift-PageUp.

INSTALLING SOFTWARE

You can install software from the command line as well as from the PIXEL menus. The Debian installation software is called APT (for Advanced Package Tool), and most of the software installation and search commands start with `apt`. You can search for packages with `aptitude search`:

```
pi@raspberrypi:~ $ aptitude search camera
p   camera.app - GNUstep application for digital still came
p   cameramonitor - Webcam monitoring in system tray
p   libomxil-bellagio0-components-c - Motorola Camera components for
    Bellagio Op
```

```
i    python-picamera - Pure Python interface to the Raspberry Pi'
p    python-picamera-docs - Documentation for the Python interface to
i    python3-picamera - Pure Python interface to the Raspberry Pi
p    python3-snap-camera - A camera that uses PiFace Control and Disp
```

The lines that start with i—python-picamera and python3-
picamera—mean those programs are already installed. The others
are available for installation. You can install them with sudo apt-
get install:

```
sudo apt-get install cameramonitor
```

APT will figure out what other packages that package
requires, and ask you whether it should install them all. If you type
y (or just press Enter), it will install all the necessary packages.

Some of the packages are downright silly. For instance, type
sudo apt-get install cowsay and then run it:

```
pi@raspberrypi:~ $ cowsay Raspberry Pi is cool
 _____
< Raspberry Pi is cool >
 ----------------------
        \   ^__^
         \  (oo)_____
            (__)\       )\/\
                ||----w |
                ||     ||
```

Another fun program is sl: it's there so that if you mean to
type ls but accidentally reverse the characters, you get something besides a boring error message. Install it and try it yourself
if you want to see what it does.

GETTING HELP

One more useful command is man, which shows the built-in
man(ual) pages. man ls tells you all about the ls command. (Press
the spacebar to advance to the next page, and press Q to quit.)
Unfortunately, a lot of the Raspbian-specific commands, like

raspi-config, don't have man pages, but you can learn a lot about basic Linux commands this way.

The apropos command helps you find man pages. So, for example, apropos gpio tells you about some man pages where you can read about the GPIO pins on the Raspberry Pi—if you didn't have this book to tell you about them.

Some commands also have built-in help. If you're wondering how to run a program, try running it with -h or --help (that's one dash with h or two dashes with help). Some of the raspi commands are nonstandard and take just help as an argument—as you'll see in the next chapter when you progress to blinking an LED.

2

Blink an LED

In the hardware world, the traditional first program most people write makes an LED blink. It's simple, and who doesn't like a light show?

The Raspberry Pi's GPIO headers let you interface with all sorts of hardware. In this chapter, you'll connect an LED to one of the GPIO pins and learn several ways of controlling it, turning it on and off and changing its brightness. You can even connect a pushbutton and modify what your LED does according to whether the button is pushed.

HARDWARE REQUIREMENTS

Here's a list of what you need for this chapter:

* An LED

* A small resistor. The exact value doesn't matter; something around 200–500 ohm is best.

* A large resistor, like 10 kΩ–100 kΩ. Again, the exact value doesn't matter.

  I strongly recommended you have the following:

* A solderless breadboard, any size

* A 2×20 pin male header you can solder to the Pi, plus a 2×20 ribbon cable

  or

* A 2×20 female header you can solder to the Pi

* Soldering equipment

  The following are optional:

* A pushbutton or switch that plugs into your breadboard

* A Pi GPIO extension, like the Adafruit Pi Cobbler or the SparkFun Pi Wedge

> **WARNING** If this is your first time soldering, practice on other components before soldering a header to the Raspberry Pi. Header pins are close together, and if you make a mistake it's not easy to recover.

WHAT IS GPIO?

Those holes down the side of the Pi Zero W are for general-purpose input/output (GPIO). That's a way of controlling hardware directly; the Pi can set pins to high or low voltages to control a device, and it can read incoming high or low voltages coming from a sensor.

But first, you've got to connect something to the GPIO.

HEADERS: HOOKING UP TO THE PI ZERO W

The Raspberry Pi Zero W is sold with bare "through-holes" for the GPIO connections, whereas larger Raspberry Pi models have pins. That makes sense—the Pi Zero line is great for hardware control, and someone buying a batch of them might want to solder wires to just a few of those connections rather than using a bulky set of pins. But it makes it a little inconvenient to start playing with your Pi Zero W.

You have several options. The classic choice is to solder a 2×20 male header, like the one shown in Figure 2.1, onto the Pi.

FIGURE 2.1: A Pi Zero W and male headers, ready to be soldered

A male header makes the Pi Zero W compatible with a wide range of add-ons sold for larger Raspberry Pi models.

If you're not comfortable with soldering, or if you eventually plan to use your Pi Zero in a very small box where there isn't room for headers, you could opt for a solderless "hammer header." These are mostly available from dealers in the United Kingdom, but Adafruit resells them in the United States.

If you use a male header, you'll need either a 40-wire ribbon cable that plugs into it or a few female-to-male wire leads.

FIGURE 2.2: Male header with female-to-male leads

You could also choose a female 2×20 pin header. It isn't as compatible with other Pi hardware, but it makes plugging in wires super easy. You don't need a ribbon cable or any special wire leads—just regular hook-up wire.

Finally, it is possible to get by temporarily without any soldering to the board if you wedge wires diagonally into the Pi's through-holes, as shown in Figure 2.3.

FIGURE 2.3: Look, Ma, no headers!

You can even use headers this way, and if you bend the ends of the wires a little where they emerge underneath the Pi Zero, they might stay in place a little better.

That said, I don't recommend working this way. The wires won't make a good connection, and you may waste time debugging projects that don't work because of a flaky connection. If you're excited to get started but don't have any 2×20 headers on hand, go ahead and try it for this chapter, but I highly recommend you order something better before you move on to Chapter 3.

In the hardware list at the beginning of this chapter, I also recommended that you get one of the Raspberry Pi GPIO extensions. These aren't necessary, but they're inexpensive and give you an easy way of making the Pi's GPIO pins accessible on a breadboard. Even better, they include labels reminding you which pin is which. They typically include a ribbon cable that connects the extension to a male header on the Pi.

FIGURE 2.4: A GPIO extension, with ribbon cable and a breadboard

WIRING AN LED ON A BREADBOARD

An LED (which stands for light-emitting diode) is an electronics component that can only pass electricity in one direction. So to hook up an LED, you have to know which pin is positive.

Most LEDs have one pin longer than the other. The long pin goes to the positive terminal, whereas the short pin goes to ground. An easy way to remember this is that the "plus" side has had some length added to it.

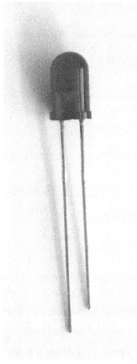

FIGURE 2.5: An LED. The long lead is the positive side.

When you wire up an LED, you should always include a resistor in the circuit to limit the current. Otherwise, too much current will flow through the LED and will probably burn it out, with a pop and a little smoke. (Ask me how I know that!)

The smaller the value of the resistor, the brighter the LED will shine. Most small LEDs only need a small resistor, around 200–500 ohms, and it's generally not critical what exact value you use.

You'll have to connect the LED to the resistor somehow. You can twist wires together or use alligator clips, but when you're

testing circuits it saves a lot of time to use a solderless breadboard (Figure 2.6).

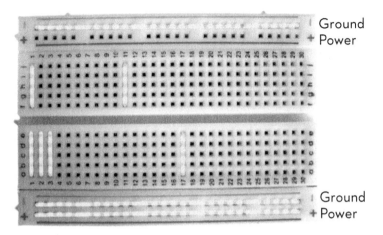

Ground
Power

Ground
Power

FIGURE 2.6: Solderless breadboard. The yellow indicates which holes are
connected.

A breadboard has rows of five holes into which you can push
wires. Each row of five holes is connected, as indicated by the
yellow lines in Figure 2.6. So if you push a lead of the resistor
and a lead of the LED into holes in the same row, they'll make
electrical contact.

Some breadboards, like the one pictured, include long strips
intended for power and ground connections. When you're building a circuit, it's fairly common to have lots of devices that need
to connect directly to power and ground, so it's useful to have the
longer strips. By convention, you'd connect the strip marked red
to power and the strip marked blue to ground. For the circuits
in this book, you won't need a power or ground strip, so any sort
of breadboard is fine.

THE RASPBERRY PI PIN LAYOUT

The Raspberry Pi's output pins are numbered starting in the upper left: pin 1 has a pad that's a square rather than a circle. The pin assignments are fairly chaotic (Figure 2.7)

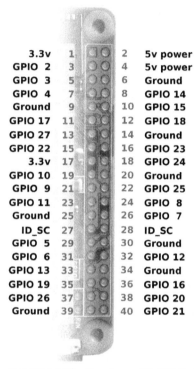

FIGURE 2.7: The Raspberry Pi's GPIO pins

So pin 1 is 3.3 volts of power, whereas pin 2 is 5 volts. Pin 3 is called GPIO 2, pin 6 is Ground, and so on to the final pin, 40, or GPIO 21. The GPIO numbers are all out of order and you aren't expected to remember this crazy layout; you might want to bookmark this page while you work on projects that use GPIO.

A Raspberry Pi can provide 5 volts of power from pins 2 and 4, but its logic circuitry (on the GPIO pins) works at 3.3 volts. If you're buying hardware you want to drive from a Pi, make sure it can work with 3.3V and doesn't require 5V. (The 5V pins are provided in case you need to power hardware that needs more than 3.3 volts.)

To test your LED circuit, connect the long lead of the LED to one of the GPIO 3.3V connections, like pin 1. Connect one lead of the resistor to a ground pin, like pin 6. Then connect the short lead of the LED to the other lead of the resistor. See Figure 2.8.

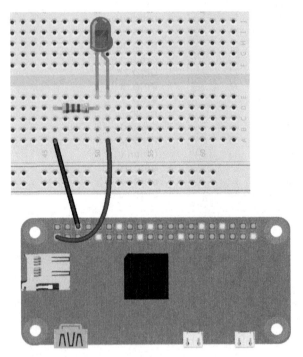

FIGURE 2.8: LED wired to 3.3V power

The LED should light up.

CONTROLLING AN LED FROM THE COMMAND LINE

Unplug your LED's positive lead from the Pi's pin 1 and connect it to GPIO 14, which is pin 8, the fourth pin in the outer row. Leave your resistor plugged into Ground. Now you're ready to control the LED from software.

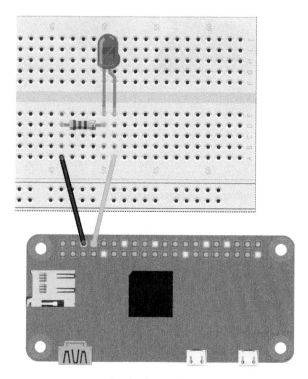

FIGURE 2.9: An LED hooked up to GPIO 14

You don't have to write any code to light an LED on a Raspberry Pi. All you need is the `raspi-gpio` command. In a terminal window connected to your Raspberry Pi, type

```
raspi-gpio set 14 op dh
```

The LED should come on.

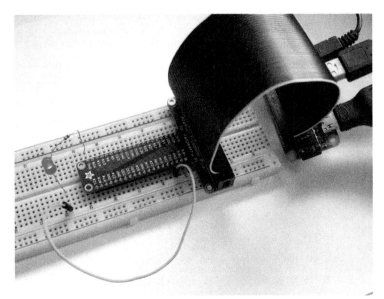

All wired up, using a Pi Cobbler extension

The pin number is 14, and the op (operation) is dh, which stands for "Driving High."

Now replace that dh with dl for "Driving Low":

```
raspi-gpio set 14 op dl
```

> TIP Remember that pressing the up arrow key will display your last shell command. Then all you have to do is press Backspace to delete the h, then type l, and press Enter.)

The LED should turn off.

That's all you need to know about raspi-gpio. But if you want the gory details, you can learn more than you ever wanted by typing

```
raspi-gpio help
```

BLINKING AN LED FROM THE COMMAND LINE

The Bash shell is programmable. You wouldn't want to write a long program in it, but it's fine for little snippets. Type the following into the shell:

```
pi@raspberrypi:~ $ while true; do
> raspi-gpio set 14 op dh
> sleep 1
> raspi-gpio set 14 op dl
> sleep 1
> done
```

> **NOTE** The > at the beginning of each line is the prompt the shell gives you; don't type that part.

You've written your first blinking LED program! First, you tell the Pi to turn on pin 14; then you tell the Pi to "sleep" (that is, not to perform any other commands) for one second. The next lines tell the Pi to turn off pin 14 and sleep for another second. The while true command tells the Pi to loop these commands. The light should blink on and off forever. That was almost too easy.

When you're tired of watching it, Ctrl-C will kill the program and give you your prompt back. (That's true of most programs in Linux.)

GPIO from the Command Line via Sysfs

There's another way to access GPIO from the command line: using an interface called *sysfs*. Sysfs lets you talk directly to the Linux kernel by writing to and reading from files.

The sysfs interface makes GPIO pins available via files inside the /sys/class/gpio directory (folder). It requires one line of setup for each pin you plan to use:

```
echo 14 > /sys/class/gpio/export
```

The echo command just prints its arguments. Adding > makes it print to a file rather than to the terminal. So this command writes 14 to the file /sys/class/gpio/export. In response, the kernel will create a new directory called /sys/class/gpio/gpio14/, containing several files you can write to control GPIO pin 14.

```
echo out > /sys/class/gpio/gpio14/direction
```

writes "out" to the file named *direction* inside the *gpio14* directory you just created. That tells the kernel you want to use that pin as output (you'd use in to use a pin for input).

```
echo 1 > /sys/class/gpio/gpio14/value
```

A value of 1 turns pin 14's voltage high (3.3 volts). The LED should go on. Echo 0 instead of 1 to turn it off again.

Of course, you can use this inside a while true; do loop, just as you did with raspi-gpio:

```
pi@raspberrypi:~ $ while true; do
> echo 1 > /sys/class/gpio/gpio14/value
> sleep 1
> echo 0 > /sys/class/gpio/gpio14/value
> sleep 1
> done
```

BLINKING AN LED FROM A PYTHON PROGRAM

Now it's time to use a real programming language: Python.

If you're using the desktop, you can run the IDLE Python development environment by choosing the following:

Menu > Programming > Python 3 (IDLE)

If you're using the command line, run the Python shell:

```
python3
```

Either way, you'll get a >>> prompt.

> **NOTE** Raspbian comes with both Python 2 and Python 3 installed. The examples in this book should work with either one, except as noted. If you're just getting started with Python, I recommend starting with 3.

Controlling an LED is easy with the GPIOzero library. Type these lines at the >>> Python prompts:

```
from gpiozero import LED
led = LED(14)
led.on()
```

You can make that into a blink program, sleeping for half a second between blinks:

```
from time import sleep
while True:
    led.on()
    sleep(.5)
    led.off()
    sleep(.5)
```

The spaces beginning each of the last four lines are important; they tell Python that the indented lines are part of the while True loop. It doesn't matter how many spaces you include as long as you use the same number for all four lines. If you use a different number of spaces, or don't indent at all, you'll get an IndentationError. The Python style guide recommends four spaces as being the most readable.

As with the shell, pressing Ctrl-C will stop the program.

Saving Your Program: Text Editors

Of course, you don't want to have to type your whole program into the Python console every time you run it. You'll want to save it to a file.

You can't use a word processor, like Word or LibreOffice, to edit programs. You need something that can edit plain text.

You have plenty of options for text editors on Linux, and Internet flame wars have been fought over which is best (most programmers prefer emacs or vim). If you don't already have a text editor you favor, try nano if you're using SSH and the command line. If you're using the graphical desktop, IDLE has a File > New option with a built-in editor, or you can use Leafpad (Accessories > Text Editor).

Save your LED blinking program to a file with a name like blink.py (you can copy and paste from the lines you typed into the Python console, or from this book's GitHub repository at *https://github.com/akkana/pi-zero-w-book*):

```
from gpiozero import LED
from time import sleep

led = LED(14)

while True:
    led.on()
    sleep(.5)
    led.off()
    sleep(.5)
```

Save the program (in IDLE or Leafpad, choose File > Save or press Ctrl-S; in nano, press Ctrl-O and then press Enter to confirm the filename). Now run it, either from IDLE's Run button or from a shell:

```
python blink.py
```

and your LED should start blinking.

FADE AN LED

The GPIOzero library also lets you set LEDs to partial brightness,
using a technique called pulse width modulation, or PWM.

A Raspberry Pi can't actually set its GPIO pins to anything
besides 1 or 0 (3.3 volts or 0 volts). What it *can* do is pulse the pin
(and therefore the LED connected to it) between 1 and 0 rapidly.
The more time it spends at 1, the brighter the LED will appear.
Fortunately, you don't have to manage this in your program; you
can let GPIOzero's PWMLED class do it for you.

Instead of creating an LED object with led = LED(14), use
PWMLED(14). Then use a variable called *value* to manage the LED's
brightness, starting at 0 and ramping up to 1, then starting again
at 0:

```
from gpiozero import PWMLED
from time import sleep

led = PWMLED(14)

value = 0
increment = .02
sleeptime = .03

try:
    while True:
        value += increment
        if value > 1:
            value = 0
        led.value = value
```

```
    sleep(sleeptime)

except KeyboardInterrupt:
    print("Bye!")
```

By the way, GPIOzero has fairly good documentation at *http://gpiozero.readthedocs.io/*. It supports a curious but incomplete collection of hardware, and in some cases it's hard to tell what hardware is needed to use specific Python classes. If you happen to be using hardware it supports, GPIOzero makes things very easy, but if you're using anything else, it won't help you.

With that in mind, it's good to know something about the more general library that sits underneath GPIOzero: RPi-gpio.

PYTHON BLINK USING RPI-GPIO

RPi-gpio has been around almost since the first Raspberry Pi, and by now it's mature and powerful. Using it directly requires a couple of lines of setup beyond that needed for GPIOzero, after which it's just as easy:

```
import RPi.GPIO as GPIO
from time import sleep

GPIO.setmode(GPIO.BCM)
GPIO.setup(14, GPIO.OUT)

while True:
    GPIO.output(14, GPIO.HIGH)
    sleep(.5)
    GPIO.output(14, GPIO.LOW)
    sleep(.5)
```

`GPIO.setmode(GPIO.BCM)` tells the RPi-gpio library to use the names of the pins. If you're using GPIO 14, you pass 14 to `GPIO.output`. BCM stands for BroadCoM, because the pin numbers come from the Broadcom-made chip used in the Raspberry Pi. The library can also use physical pin numbers, if you pass BOARD instead of BCM. If you look at the pin diagram in Figure 2.7, GPIO 14 is on physical pin 8, so this would also have worked:

```
GPIO.setmode(GPIO.BOARD)
GPIO.setup(8, GPIO.OUT)
GPIO.output(8, GPIO.HIGH)
```

You may see a warning like `blink-rpi-gpio.py:8: Runtime-Warning: This channel is already in use, continuing anyway. Use GPIO.setwarnings(False) to disable warnings.` You'd see this warning if the other programs you've been running didn't clean up after themselves. When they stopped using the Pi's GPIO, they left the GPIO pins active, potentially causing problems for programs that might run later.

Ideally, you should clean up after your program has run, but interrupting it with Ctrl-C makes that more difficult. You could avoid the Ctrl-C by blinking only a fixed number of times, instead of forever:

```
for i in range(10):
    GPIO.output(14, GPIO.HIGH)
    sleep(.5)
    GPIO.output(14, GPIO.LOW)
    sleep(.5)

GPIO.cleanup()
```

Note that the GPIO.cleanup() line isn't indented. That way, Python knows it's not part of the loop, and it won't run until the ten blink cycles have finished.

If you want to keep the infinite loop and interrupt it with Ctrl-C as you've been doing but still clean up afterward, you could "catch" the interrupt like this:

```
import RPi.GPIO as GPIO
from time import sleep

GPIO.setmode(GPIO.BCM)
GPIO.setup(14, GPIO.OUT)
```

```
try:
    while True:
        GPIO.output(14, GPIO.HIGH)
        sleep(.5)
        GPIO.output(14, GPIO.LOW)
        sleep(.5)

except KeyboardInterrupt:
    GPIO.cleanup()
```

You could have caught KeyboardInterrupt in your earlier GPIOzero blink program, and GPIOzero would have cleaned up automatically. With GPIOzero, you don't have to call a cleanup function explicitly; just add pass inside the except section to make sure the keyboard interrupt was caught.

```
try:
    while True:
        led.on()
        sleep(.5)
        led.off()
        sleep(.5)
except KeyboardInterrupt:
    pass
```

PYTHON FADE USING RPI-GPIO

Of course you can fade with RPi-gpio PWM as well. Anything to the right of a # character is a Python comment and not part of the running code.

```
import RPi.GPIO as GPIO
from time import sleep

GPIO.setmode(GPIO.BCM)

GPIO.setup(14, GPIO.OUT)
pwm = GPIO.PWM(14, 100)         # Set up PWM on pin 14 at 100 Hz

value = 0
pwm.start(value)                # Start at 0
```

```
increment = 2                 # How smooth is the fade?
sleeptime = .03               # How fast is the fade?

try:
    while True:
        value += increment
        if value > 100:
            value = 0
        pwm.ChangeDutyCycle(value)
        sleep(sleeptime)

except KeyboardInterrupt:
    pwm.stop()
    GPIO.cleanup()
```

READING INPUT: A PUSHBUTTON

You can read input from pins with RPi-gpio as well as set pin values.

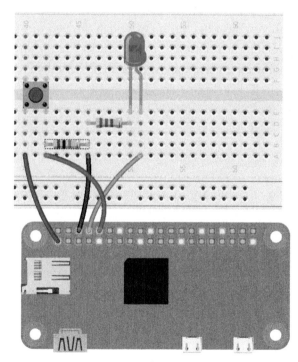

FIGURE 2.11: Wiring an LED plus a pushbutton. Notice that both resistors are tied to Ground on the Pi.

Leave your LED connected, and wire up a pushbutton. If you don't have a pushbutton handy or can't find one that plugs into your breadboard, you can fake it using two bare wires that you'll touch together. That's really all a pushbutton is.

1. Wire one side of the button to pin 1, 3.3v power.

2. Wire the other side of the button to pin 10, GPIO 15. Then attach a high-value resistor, like 10 kΩ or more, to that same side of the switch. The other side of the resistor goes to ground.

This is what's known as a "pull-down" resistor. Without the resistor, when the switch is open, GPIO 15 isn't connected to anything. It's not definitely high or definitely low, so if you read its value, there's no telling what you might see. With the resistor in place, if the switch is open, GPIO is tied to ground through the resistor. But when you push the button (or touch the two wires together if you don't have a button), it's much easier for current to flow from the 3.3v pin through the switch to GPIO 15 than to go through that big 10 kΩ resistor. So GPIO 15 reads high.

Now you can read the value at GPIO 15 from Python:

```
GPIO.setup(15, GPIO.IN)

print("button:" + GPIO.input(buttonpin))
```

Let's try doing something with it in the blinking loop. For instance, you could make the LED blink slowly most of the time, but make it blink faster when you press the button.

To make the code a little cleaner, I'll make variables for the LED pin and the button pin—that makes it easier to change them if you decide to use different pins—and for the sleep durations.

Here's the program written for GPIOzero:

```
from gpiozero import LED, Button
```

```
from time import sleep

led = LED(14)
button = Button(15)

# Blink times in seconds:
shortblink = .1
longblink = .7

for i in range(100):
    # Set the LED pin to high for odd numbers, low for even.
    if i % 2:
        led.on()
    else:
        led.off()

    if button.is_pressed:
        sleep(shortblink)
    else:
        sleep(longblink)
```

The program loops 100 times. `i % 2` is called a modulo—it divides `i` by 2 and takes the remainder. So when `i` is odd, `i % 2` will be 1, and the LED will come on. When `i` is even, `i % 2` will be 0 and the LED will turn off.

Then each time around, if the button is pressed, we'll only sleep for a short time; if the button isn't pressed, we'll sleep longer.

Here's an RPi-gpio version:

```
import RPi.GPIO as GPIO
from time import sleep

# Use Raspberry Pi board pin numbers:
GPIO.setmode(GPIO.BCM)

ledpin = 14
buttonpin = 15

# Blink times in seconds:
shortblink = .1
longblink = .7
```

```
# set up GPIO output channel
GPIO.setup(ledpin, GPIO.OUT)
GPIO.setup(buttonpin, GPIO.IN)

for i in range(100):
    # Set the LED pin to high for odd numbers, low for even.
    if i % 2:
        GPIO.output(ledpin, GPIO.HIGH)
    else:
        GPIO.output(ledpin, GPIO.LOW)

    # Sleep for a short time if the button is pressed, otherwise a
long time:
    if GPIO.input(buttonpin):
        sleep(shortblink)
    else:
        sleep(longblink)

# Done: clean up!
GPIO.cleanup()
```

OTHER LANGUAGES, OTHER INTERFACES

There are lots of options for programming the GPIO on a Raspberry Pi. You've already seen a shell script and Python. But if you have another favorite language, don't despair: you can control the Pi's GPIO from C or C++, Ruby, Perl, Java, C#, Pascal, BASIC, Gambas (similar to Visual Basic), and even Scratch. There's no shortage of options!

Now you have the basics of both input and output with the Raspberry Pi's GPIO. LEDs and switches are simple, but a lot of hardware works pretty much the same way.

But some hardware is more complicated. In Chapters 3 and 4, we'll take a look at interfacing with other types of hardware, as well as some things you can do with the Zero W's Wi-Fi capabilities.

3

A Temperature Notifier and Fan Control

Do you hate to come home to a hot house? Or do you just want to know what the temperature is in your office so you can dress appropriately?

In this project, you'll set up your Pi to monitor the temperature and make it available via Twitter. The Pi can even turn on a fan or an air conditioner before you get home, based on temperature limits you set or a Twitter message you send it.

HARDWARE REQUIREMENTS

Here's a list of what you need for this chapter:

* An I²C temperature sensor, such as the Si7021, MCP9808, or BME280

* Four hookup wires

* A PowerSwitch Tail (optional, for switching on a fan or air conditioner)

FIGURE 3.1: Testing an automated fan with a PowerSwitch Tail and three different temperature sensors on the I²C bus

> **NOTE** If you want to copy and paste rather than typing the code by hand, you can find working examples at the book's GitHub repository: *https://github.com/akkana/pi-zero-w-book*. You can even check it out on your Pi: git clone *https://github .com/akkana/pi-zero-w-book.git*.

The first thing you'll need is a temperature sensor board. These are inexpensive, around $5 to $10, depending on accuracy and the other features they offer, such as the ability to measure humidity or barometric pressure. Most of them use a protocol called I²C.

WHAT IS I²C?

I²C (pronounced "eye squared see" or "eye two see") stands for inter-integrated circuit. It's a protocol for reading information from, and writing to, low-power devices like sensors. It uses two wires (for clock and data) plus another pair for power and ground. You'll sometimes see references to "two-wire" interfaces, which are more or less the same thing as I²C.

Each I²C device has an address, and you can have multiple devices connected to your Pi at the same time as long as they have different addresses.

The System Management Bus (SMBus) is a slightly simpler subset of I²C. That's worth knowing mostly because one of the ways of talking to I²C devices using Python is called *smbus*. The smbus library is fairly simple to use despite an almost complete lack of documentation; fortunately, you can find lots of examples on the web. (The GPIOzero library has no support—yet—for I²C. RPi-gpio has some support, but it's a lot more fiddly than smbus.)

If you're using Raspbian-lite, you'll have to install a couple of packages first. On the full version of Raspbian, these packages are probably already installed, but it doesn't hurt to run this command anyway to be sure:

```
sudo apt-get install i2c-tools python-smbus
```

Enabling I²C

Raspbian comes with support for I²C built in, but it's disabled by default. Fortunately, it's easy to enable.

In a terminal, type **sudo raspi-config**, move down to Interfacing Options, and press Enter. Then move down to I2C and press Enter again. Use the Tab or left-arrow key and press Enter to answer Yes to "Would you like the ARM I²C interface to be enabled?"

Or, if you prefer using the GUI, choose Preferences > Raspberry Pi Configuration and click the OK button to enable I²C.

Either way, once you exit you should have I²C enabled. To verify that, in a terminal, type this:

```
ls /dev/i2c*
```

Note the asterisk at the end of the command: it's a wildcard that means you want to show any file in /dev that starts with i2c. The Pi should respond with this:

```
/dev/i2c-1
```

If you see /dev/i2c-1, you're set. (On early Raspberry Pis, it was called i2c-0 instead of 1.)

If you see i2cdetect: command not found, it means you didn't install i2c-tools and python-smbus (see the section "What Is I²C?" earlier).

CHOOSING A SENSOR

A wide variety of inexpensive temperature sensors are available that "speak" I²C. Since the chips themselves are tiny, they're often available mounted on "breakout boards" that make it easy to plug the sensor into a breadboard and wire it to your Raspberry Pi. Many temperature sensors also measure other quantities, such as atmospheric pressure or humidity.

Whichever sensor you choose, you'll need to figure out how to talk to it from the Pi. Each I²C device has a different address and speaks a slightly different language. The details for each chip are in its *datasheet* (a PDF that you can find with a web search; for example, search for "Si7021 datasheet"), but extracting the details from a datasheet isn't always easy. I recommend starting with a web search for the chip name plus "python" or even "raspberry pi python" to see if someone has already done that work for you. Ideally, do this before you order a sensor, so you'll know ahead of time if a sensor is difficult to use with Python on the Pi.

Let's start with the simple and accurate MCP9808 chip.

The MCP9808 I²C Temperature Sensor

The breakout board has eight holes, but you'll only need four of them for basic I²C: Vdd (input voltage, 3.3 volts), Gnd (ground), SCL (clock), and SDA (data).

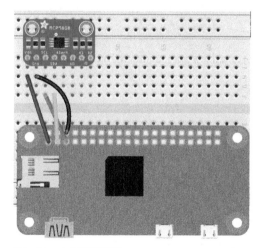

FIGURE 3.2: MCP9808 temperature sensor wiring

You'll probably need to solder a header onto your breakout board, or use test leads with clips that can make good contact with the through-holes on the board.

If you have hookup wires in a selection of colors, I suggest a color code convention: use red for power, black for ground, orange or yellow for clock (remember this as "clock works orange"), and green or blue for data. If you don't have that many wire colors, don't worry—the Pi and the chip won't care; a color code just makes it easier for humans to see at a glance what's wired to what.

On the Pi Zero end, wire the 3.3v power (red) wire to pin 1 on the Pi, and the ground (black) wire to any of the Pi's ground connections, such as pin 6 or pin 9. Refer to Figure 2.7, in the previous chapter, if you need to check pin numbers. Wire SDA to the Pi's pin 3 (GPIO 2), and CLK (clock) to pin 5 (GPIO 3).

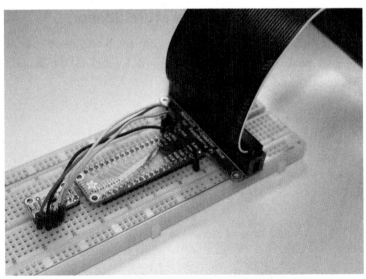

FIGURE 3.3: MCP9808 wired up to the Pi Zero W, ready to test

Now check to make sure your Pi sees the new I²C device. In a shell, type

```
pi@raspberrypi:~ $ i2cdetect -y 1
```

In that command, 1 is the number of the I²C bus you're using. Modern Raspberry Pis, including the Zero W, have two I²C buses, and bus 1 uses pins 3 and 5; older Pis have only one, bus 0.

You should see the following:

```
     0    1  2  3  4  5  6  7  8  9  a  b  c  d  e  f
00:            -- -- -- -- -- -- -- -- -- -- -- -- --
10: -- -- -- -- -- -- -- -- 18 -- -- -- -- -- -- --
20: -- -- -- -- -- -- -- -- -- -- -- -- -- -- -- --
30: -- -- -- -- -- -- -- -- -- -- -- -- -- -- -- --
40: -- -- -- -- -- -- -- -- -- -- -- -- -- -- -- --
50: -- -- -- -- -- -- -- -- -- -- -- -- -- -- -- --
60: -- -- -- -- -- -- -- -- -- -- -- -- -- -- -- --
```

The output shows that the Pi detected a device at address (10 + 8) = 18—the address the MCP9808 uses. If you don't see anything there, check your wiring and don't proceed until `ic2detect -y 1` gives the right output. If you see a number other than 18 and you don't have anything else plugged into your Pi, it might be that your MCP9808 is using a different address; try using the address you see instead of 0x18 when you write your program.

If you're sure your wires are plugged into all the right places but `i2cdetect` still doesn't see the sensor, try connecting A0, A1, and A2 on the sensor to ground on the Pi. Those lines set the address of the MCP9808, and some breakout boards may need the address lines grounded.

Measuring the Temperature

You can read data from an I²C device with smbus:

```
import smbus
bus = smbus.SMBus(1)
bus.read_i2c_block_data(address, cmd)
```

For this sensor, *address* is 18 in base 16. In Python, you can represent a hexadecimal number by putting *Ox* in front of it, so it's *Ox18*. *cmd* is the command you're sending to the chip to tell it to give you a temperature reading: for the MCP9808, that's 0x05.

The trick is interpreting the bytes it sends back. The MCP9808 sends 2 bytes (data[0] and data[1] in the Python code), and its datasheet helpfully gives example code to translate these 2 bytes into a temperature in Celsius. Translated into Python, that code sample looks like this:

```python
# Read temperature from an MCP9808 using I2C.

import smbus

MCP9808 = 0x18        # The default I2C address of the MCP9808
temp_reg = 0x05       # The temperature register

bus = smbus.SMBus(1)

def read_temperature_c():
    data = bus.read_i2c_block_data(MCP9808, temp_reg)

    # Calculate temperature (see 5.1.3.1 in the datasheet):
    upper_byte = data[0] & 0x1f    # clear flag bits
    lower_byte = data[1]
    if upper_byte & 0x10 == 0x10:  # less than 0C
        upper_byte &= 0x0f
        return 256 - (upper_byte * 16.0 + lower_byte / 16.0)
    else:
        return upper_byte * 16.0 + lower_byte / 16.0

if __name__ == '__main__':
    ctemp = read_temperature_c()
    ftemp = ctemp * 1.8 +32
    print("Temperature: %.2f F (%.2f C)" % ftemp, ctemp)
```

Run it, either from IDLE or in the shell:

```
python MCP9808.py
```

and it should print the temperature in both Fahrenheit and Celsius.

Here's one more neat feature of the MCP9808: it can use addresses besides 0x18. That's what those extra pins on the board are for. So if you want to have multiple MCP9808 sensors attached to your Pi at the same time, you can—as long as you wire their addresses so they're all different.

Measuring Temperature and Humidity with an Si7021

Another popular sensor is the Si7021, which measures humidity as well as temperature. It has an older sibling, the HTU21d, that uses the same address and works with the same code. Its hookup is similar to the MCP9808 and it uses the same four wires: power, ground, data, and clock. You can see a wiring diagram in Figure 3.4.

FIGURE 3.4: Si7021 temperature and humidity sensor

The software side is a little more complicated than the other chip, since the Si7021 handles several commands. Aside from measuring both temperature and humidity, it has "hold" and "no hold" modes.

But that's just the start of the problems. It turns out that when you read 2 bytes from an Si7021 using the smbus library, the second byte is always the same as the first. So you're really only reading one byte, and you won't get the full accuracy of the chip.

> NOTE When you work with hardware, you'll hit problems like this all too often. Chips don't do quite what they claim, documentation is missing, libraries have bugs, and quirks need to be worked around. That's all normal, and if you start feeling a little frustrated, don't feel like it's just you.

The duplicated byte seems to be a bug in the smbus library, and I never did find a way to get smbus to read that second byte. Fortunately, there are other solutions. For instance, you can read from and write to the /dev/i2c-1 device directly, and use an interface called fcntl (short for "file control").

Here's a program that does that:

```python
import time, array
import io, fcntl

class Si7021:
    ADDRESS = 0x40
    I2C_SLAVE=0x0703
    READ_TEMP_NOHOLD = b"\xF3"
    READ_HUM_NOHOLD = b"\xF5"
    SOFT_RESET = b"\xFE"

    def __init__(self, bus):
        # Open the I2C bus:
        self.fread  = io.open("/dev/i2c-%d" % bus, "rb",
                              buffering=0)
        self.fwrite = io.open("/dev/i2c-%d" % bus, "wb",
                              buffering=0)

        # initialize the device as a slave:
        fcntl.ioctl(self.fread, self.I2C_SLAVE, self.ADDRESS)
        fcntl.ioctl(self.fwrite, self.I2C_SLAVE, self.ADDRESS)
```

```python
        self.fwrite.write(self.SOFT_RESET)
        time.sleep(.1)

    def close(self):
        self.fread.close()
        self.fwrite.close()

    def readI2C(self, cmd):
        self.fwrite.write(cmd)
        time.sleep(.1)

        data = self.fread.read(3)
        buf = array.array('B', data)

        if self.crc8check(buf):
            return buf
        else:
            return None

    def read_temperature_c(self):
        buf = self.readI2C(self.READ_TEMP_NOHOLD)
        if not buf:
            return -273.15    # absolute zero

        return (((buf[0] << 8 | buf [1]) & 0xFFFC)
            * 175.72 / 65536.0 - 46.85)

    def read_humidity(self):
        buf = self.readI2C(self.READ_HUM_NOHOLD)
        if not buf:
            return -1

        return (((buf[0] << 8 | buf [1]) & 0xFFFC)
            * 125.0 / 65536.0 - 6.0)

    def crc8check(self, value):
        remainder = ( ( value[0] << 8 ) + value[1] ) << 8
        remainder |= value[2]
        divisor = 0x988000

        for i in range(0, 16):
            if( remainder & 1 << (23 - i) ):
                remainder ^= divisor
            divisor = divisor >> 1
```

```
        if remainder == 0:
            return True
        else:
            return False

if __name__ == '__main__':
    sensor = Si7021(1)
    ctemp = sensor.read_temperature_c()
    print("Temperature:  %.2f F (%.2f C)"
        % ctemp * 1.8 + 32, ctemp)
    print("Relative Humidity: %.1f %%"
        % sensor.read_humidity())
    sensor.close()
```

Reading Temperature and Pressure from a BME280

The final temperature sensor we'll cover here is the BME280, which lets you read barometric pressure as well as temperature. The pressure sensor is said to be accurate enough that you can use it as an altimeter—though for that, you'd need to calibrate it, since air pressure varies according to the weather as well as with altitude.

It wires up pretty much the same as the other two chips, as you can see in Figure 3.5.

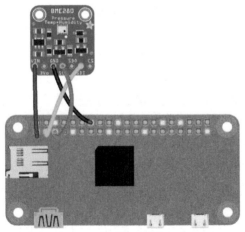

FIGURE 3.5: Wiring the BME280 temperature and pressure sensor

However, in software the BME is quite a bit more complicated than the other two sensors. It needs to be initialized, and then you have to read several values and turn them into temperature and pressure.

Fortunately, other people have already done that for you, and there are several libraries that work well. So rather than trying to reproduce pages of code here, do a web search for "raspberry pi python bme280," or check this book's GitHub repo, *https://github.com/akkana/pi-zero-w-book*, for example code that you can use with the BME280.

A TEMPERATURE TWEETER

One of the nifty features of the Raspberry Pi Zero W is that it has WiFi built in. So you could, say, set up a Twitter account to tweet the temperature.

Registering with Twitter

The hard work is registration. In order to use Twitter from a program, you have to register your program with Twitter and jump through some hoops to set up what's known as *OAuth authentication*.

Go to *https://apps.twitter.com/* (on any computer—you don't have to do this part on the Pi), log in to Twitter if you haven't already, and click Create New App. If you're setting up a special Twitter account for your temperature tweeter, log in as that account rather than your normal account.

> NOTE Registering a Twitter app requires registering a mobile phone number with Twitter. If that's not an option, you won't be able to use the Twitter API. In that case, skip ahead to "Controlling a Fan or Air Conditioner."

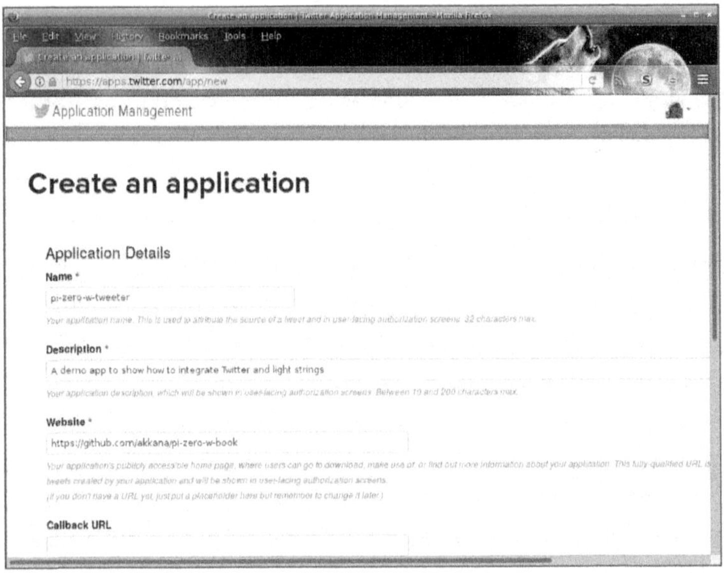

FIGURE 3.6: Twitter's page for registering a new app

In the Application Details page, the hard part is the first entry, *Name*. Your app name has to be unique in the universe of everyone who's ever registered a Twitter app. You may have to try quite a few times to come up with a name no one else has ever thought of. Good luck!

The rest of the fields are easier. *Description* is a short description of what your app does. When you're first registering it, you probably don't know yet what it will do, so this isn't too critical. You can change it later. *Website* is a URL for a website describing the app. If you have a web page or a GitHub repository where you'll describe it, use that. If not, make something up.

Callback URL applies mostly to web apps; you can leave it blank for a Python app.

Of course, you have to click that you've read the Developer Agreement and understood all the clauses about firstborn children and blood sacrifices. You did notice those parts, right?

Click Create Your Twitter Application. If you found a name that's not taken, Twitter will take you to the Application Settings page. Otherwise, try another name.

In Application Settings, click the Permissions tab and check the access permissions; by default, the setting may be Read or Read, Write but you may want to change it to Read, Write and Access Direct Messages. (In Chapter 4, you will use Twitter's direct messages.) Changing the permissions will change your secret keys, so set the permissions first.

The secret keys? They're the point of this whole exercise. Once you have the permissions the way you want them, click the Keys And Access Tokens tab at the top of the page.

You'll see Consumer Key and Consumer Secret there. But you need two other tokens as well: Access Token and Access Token Secret. Even though it sounds like some of them are secret and some aren't, all four of the tokens are secret and you shouldn't put them in your Python program or share them with other people.

To generate the other two tokens, scroll down and click "Create my access token" at the bottom of page.

FIGURE 3.7: Click "Create my access token" to generate the third and fourth tokens.

Now you're on a page that shows all four tokens. Copy and paste them to a file. Linux generally stores configurations in directories named ~/.config/*APPNAME*/ (on Linux, the tilde character, ~, is short for your home directory, /home/pi, so this is really /home/pi/.config/APPNAME). Create that directory. Then, from the shell, type

```
mkdir ~/.config/YOUR_APP_NAME
```

Replace *YOUR_APP_NAME* appropriately (but it's best to avoid using spaces).

Then in your editor, create a file in that directory called auth. For instance, if you're using nano to edit files, use this:

```
nano ~/.config/YOUR_APP_NAME/auth
```

Store your four Twitter tokens in it so it looks like this:

```
consumer YOUR_CONSUMER_KEY
consumer_secret YOUR_CONSUMER_SECRET_KEY
access_token YOUR_ACCESS_TOKEN
access_token_secret YOUR_SECRET_ACCESS_TOKEN
```

Of course, replace *YOUR_CONSUMER_KEY* and the other three variables with the actual keys you copy from the Twitter page.

Now your Python programs will be able to read the keys from that file without any risk of people seeing your secret keys when you share your code.

Python Twitter Libraries

There are lots of Python wrappers for the Twitter API. The two most popular are Python-Twitter and Tweepy. They're similar enough that if you learn one, you can probably learn the other without too much difficulty. I'll use Python-Twitter here. Install it with this command:

```
sudo apt-get install python-twitter
```

If you prefer to use the graphical installer in PIXEL, that's fine too.

> **NOTE** The Python-Twitter in the Raspbian repositories only works with Python 2, which is the default Python in Raspbian. If you prefer Python 3, you'll need to install Python-Twitter with pip3.

Python-Twitter depends on several other packages. The installer will ask you to confirm that it's okay to install those packages too.

You're ready to start coding. At the beginning of your temperature-sensing program, import the `twitter` module (that's Python-Twitter, which you just installed). Read in the four tokens from the file, examining each line to figure out which token is which and storing them in a dictionary called *oauthtokens*. Then call `twitter.Api()` to log in and get a `twitter.Api` object.

```
import twitter

def init_twitter():
    conffile = "/home/pi/.config/YOUR_APP_NAME/auth"
    oauthtokens = {}
    with open(conffile) as conf:
        for line in conf:
            line = line.split()
            oauthtokens[line[0]] = line[1]

    return twitter.Api(
        consumer_key=oauthtokens["consumer"],
        consumer_secret=oauthtokens["consumer_secret"],
        access_token_key=oauthtokens["access_token"],
        access_token_secret=oauthtokens["access_token_secret"])
```

Once you're logged in, you can call Twitter functions to get the timeline, check direct messages, post tweets, and so forth. At first, though, all you'll need is the ability to post a new tweet.

Tweeting the Temperature

If you've already initialized the Twitter API, all you need to post a tweet is PostUpdate("*Whatever you want to say*"). You can easily add that to your temperature monitoring program:

```
if __name__ == '__main__':
    twitapi = init_twitter()

    ctemp = read_temperature_c()
    ftemp = ctemp * 1.8 + 32
    twitapi.PostUpdate("The temperature is %.1f degrees!" % ftemp)
```

In practice, though, this approach can fail in various ways. For instance, if you run this code inside a while True loop and the temperature hasn't changed since last time, you'll be trying to post the exact same tweet as last time, and your program will die with a Twitter error, since Twitter assumes that if you try to post the same tweet twice, it must be a mistake. To guard against that, check for Twitter exceptions:

```
while True:
    ctemp = read_temperature_c()
    ftemp = ctemp * 1.8 + 32
    try:
        tempx = "The temperature is %.1f degrees!"
        twitapi.PostUpdate(tempx % ftemp)
    except twitter.TwitterError as e:
        print("Twitter error: %s" % str(e))
```

Of course, you can do variations, such as posting only if the temperature is above a certain value:

```
    try:
        if ftemp>90:
            tempx = "It's too hot!! %.1f degrees!"
            twitapi.PostUpdate(tempx % ftemp)
    except twitter.TwitterError as e:
        print("Twitter error: %s" % str(e))
```

CONTROLLING A FAN OR AIR CONDITIONER

In Chapter 2, "Blink an LED," you turned LEDs on and off. But what if you want to control something big? For instance, wouldn't it be nice to be able to switch on your air conditioner automatically when the temperature rises above 85 degrees?

You can't do that directly; if you tried to send 120 volts of alternating current through a Raspberry Pi you'd have crispy burned Pi. You need something that can take input at one voltage and use it to switch a circuit running at a completely different voltage. You can buy relays that will do the job, but there's a device that makes it much easier: the PowerSwitch Tail (see Figure 3.8).

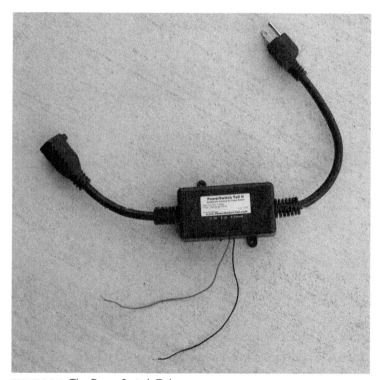

FIGURE 3.8: The PowerSwitch Tail

The manufacturer calls the PowerSwitch Tail "an opto-isolated solid-state relay." The important part of that is "isolated"; it means there's no electrical connection between the 120-volt AC your house devices use and the delicate 3.3–5-volt DC innards of your Raspberry Pi. (And yes, there's a 220-volt version for use outside the United States.)

To wire up the PowerSwitch Tail, you'll need two or three bare wires and a slim flat-bladed screwdriver to anchor the wires. On the Pi Zero W, use the same pin you used for the LED in Chapter 2: pin 8 or GPIO 14 (though nearly any GPIO pin will work).

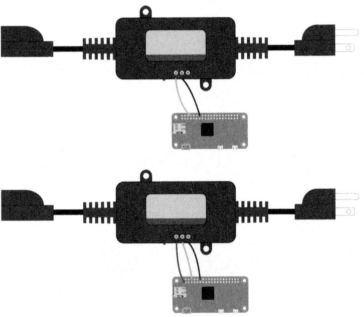

FIGURE 3.9: Two ways of wiring the PowerSwitch Tail

The PowerSwitch Tail has three terminals, labeled *+in*, *-in*, and *Ground*. There are two ways to hook it up. First, you can connect *-in* to a ground connection on your Pi, and connect *+in* to the GPIO signal line you'll control with software. A second option is to connect *Ground* on the PowerSwitch Tail to ground on the Pi, connect *+in* to 3.3v on the Pi, and connect *-in* to your GPIO line.

Whichever route you choose, set the GPIO line to high or low the same way you did with the blinking LED in Chapter 2. Depending on what model of PowerSwitch Tail you have, the logic may be reversed; you might need to set the GPIO line to high to make AC flow through the PowerSwitch Tail, or you might need to set it to low.

You don't need to have anything plugged in to the Power-Switch Tail to test it; it has an LED that lights up when power would be flowing, and you can hear it click whenever it switches on or off. You can test it with your LED code from Chapter 2—except now, instead of controlling a single LED, you can control a desk lamp, fan, air conditioner, or anything else you can plug into house current. Of course, with a fan or air conditioner, you probably don't want to blink it on and off every second!

Switching a Fan Automatically by Temperature

I'll use the MCP9808 sensor since its code is the smallest, but you can replace the code inside get_temperature_f() with code for any sensor you have.

```
# Control a fan or air conditioner using temperature sensor readings

import RPi.GPIO as GPIO
import smbus
from time import sleep

# Constants:
MCP9808 = 0x18        # The default I2C address of the MCP9808
TEMP_REG = 0x05       # The temperature register
POWERSWITCH = 14      # GPIO pin for the PowerSwitch Tail

# Depending on your model, you might need to reverse these:
FAN_ON = GPIO.HIGH
```

```
FAN_OFF = GPIO.LOW

# How hot does it have to get before turning on a fan?
TOO_HOT = 80

# How many seconds should we sleep between temp checks?
SLEEPTIME = 60 * 5

bus = smbus.SMBus(1)

def initialize():
    GPIO.setmode(GPIO.BCM)
    GPIO.setup(POWERSWITCH, GPIO.OUT)

def get_temperature_f():
    '''Return temperature in Fahrenheit'''
    data = bus.read_i2c_block_data(MCP9808, TEMP_REG)

    # Calculate temperature (see 5.1.3.1 in the datasheet):
    upper_byte = data[0] & 0x1f    # clear flag bits
    lower_byte = data[1]
    if upper_byte & 0x10 == 0x10:  # less than 0C
        upper_byte &= 0x0f
        ctemp = 256 - (upper_byte * 16.0 + lower_byte / 16.0)
    else:
        ctemp = upper_byte * 16.0 + lower_byte / 16.0


    print(ctemp * 1.8 + 32)
    return ctemp * 1.8 + 32

if __name__ == '__main__':
    initialize()

    try:
        while True:
            temp = get_temperature_f()
            if temp >= TOO_HOT:
                GPIO.output(POWERSWITCH, FAN_ON)
            else:
                GPIO.output(POWERSWITCH, FAN_OFF)

            sleep(SLEEPTIME)
    except KeyboardInterrupt:
        GPIO.cleanup()
```

Adjust the constants as needed, like which pins you're using, whether you need a HIGH or LOW signal to turn your fan on, and what temperature should trigger the fan to come on.

Switching via Internet Messaging

If you don't want to use automatic temperature sensing, you can send a message over the Internet to switch your AC on and off remotely from work or wherever you might be. I'll use Twitter messaging as an example, but you could check email messages, or use a service that receives SMS messages you send from your phone.

For instance, you could send your Pi a direct message with a special code, like "FAN ON." Then your Pi could check for messages inside the code from the earlier listing in the section "Tweeting the Temperature." Add import calendar to the Python imports at the top of the file, and then add a check_for_command function:

```
import twitter
import calendar
import time
import RPi.GPIO as GPIO

def init_twitter():
    # THE SAME CODE YOU USED IN PREVIOUS EXAMPLES

twitapi = init_twitter()
messages_seen = set()

def check_for_command(twitapi, code, recentminutes):
    '''Check for the last msg that starts with code
        and was sent in the specified number of minutes.
        Look for the command after the code, e.g., FAN ON.
        Returns (cmd, user) if there was a command,
        cmd is a string like "ON", user is a screen name.
        Returns (None, None) if there was no command.
    '''
    DMs = twitapi.GetDirectMessages(count=5, skip_status=True)
    now = time.time()
    for msg in DMs:
```

```
            # Have we already seen this message?
            if msg.id in messages_seen:
                break
            messages_seen.add(msg.id)

            if msg.text.startswith(code):
                # strip off the code part to get the ON or OFF command:
                cmd = msg.text[len(code):].strip()

                # Parse the creation time for the message,
                # make sure it was sent recently
                t = time.strptime(msg.created_at,
                                  '%a %b %d %H:%M:%S +0000 %Y')
                # How old is the message?
                minutesold = (now - calendar.timegm(t)) / 60
                if minutesold > recentminutes:
                    break

                # We have a valid command.
                return cmd, msg.sender_screen_name

    # Didn't see a command:
    return None, None
```

A lot of the code has to do with parsing the time to be sure
you're not responding to a command you sent three weeks ago.
Twitter sends times that look like "Wed Jul 05 19:15:12 +0000
2017" in GMT, so you have to turn that into a Python time in order
to compare it to the current time.

You'll probably want to add some extra checking inside the
`if msg.text.startswith(code)` section for security, to make sure
the message comes from your account. You don't want just any
Twitter user to be able to message your Pi and switch your home
appliances on or off!

Add the Twitter code to your PowerSwitch Tail program, and
in the `while True:` loop, instead of (or in addition to) checking
whether `temp >= TOO_HOT`, check for a Twitter message:

```
if __name__ == '__main__':
    twitapi = init_twitter()
```

```
powerswitch = 14
GPIO.setmode(GPIO.BCM)
GPIO.setup(powerswitch, GPIO.OUT)

try:
    while True:
        cmd, user = check_for_command(twitapi, "FAN", 30)
        if cmd == "ON":
            GPIO.output(powerswitch, GPIO.HIGH)
            twitapi.PostDirectMessage("Turned fan ON",
                                    screen_name=user)
        elif cmd == "OFF":
            GPIO.output(powerswitch, GPIO.LOW)
            twitapi.PostDirectMessage("Turned fan OFF",
                                    screen_name=user)
        elif cmd:
            twitapi.PostDirectMessage("Unknown command %s"
                                    % cmd,
                                    screen_name=user)

        time.sleep(60 * 5)    # sleep 5 minutes between checks

except KeyboardInterrupt:
    GPIO.cleanup()
```

Then all you have to do is send yourself (or your Pi, if you've set up a different Twitter account for it) a direct message saying "FAN ON," and the Pi will see the ON command and switch on the fan for you, and then message you back to tell you it saw the command. If you want to turn it off again, send another message, "FAN OFF."

Pretty cool—literally!

4

A Wearable News Alert Light Show

You know how to make a single LED blink. By using several GPIO pins, you could make a few LEDs blink together. But how about a ring of twelve multicolored LEDs, or a string of thirty, all changing colors at once? That makes for a much prettier light display—especially when you can pin it on your jacket or wear it as a belt, which is no problem with a computer as small and power efficient as the Pi Zero W.

This chapter will introduce a couple of kinds of addressable colored LEDs and show how to wire, power, and program them. You'll be able to monitor your Twitter feed and change the pattern of the lights according to what's happening on Twitter. Or, if you don't use Twitter, you can scrape any website you follow and display it as a light show.

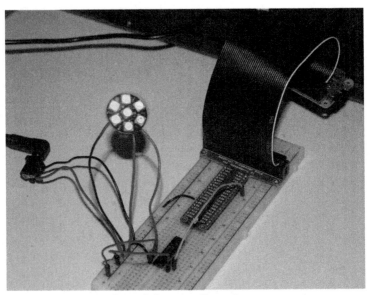

FIGURE 4.1: A NeoPixel Jewel showing off its colors

HARDWARE REQUIREMENTS

Here's a list of what you need for this chapter:

* An addressable RGB light string. There are two types: the WS2812B or the SK6812, sold under the name "NeoPixel," and a newer type, the APA102C, sold by Adafruit under the name "DotStar." DotStars are a little more expensive and aren't available in as many shapes, but they're easier to use and capable of more lighting effects.

* A power supply for the lights, with a jack to match its plug. You can get a plug-in "wall wart," a battery if you want to make it wearable, or both. See "Power Supplies" in a moment, or check out the section "Making It Portable: Batteries" at the end of this chapter if you want battery details.

* A 3.3- to 5-volt active level shifter chip such as a 74AHCT125 or a 74AHCT245. You can get by without a level shifter, but if you're ordering parts and paying for shipping any-way, spend the extra buck and a half and buy one. See the section "Logic Level Shifters" later in this chapter for more information.

* Soldering equipment. Most light strings come without wires attached, so you'll have to solder on some wires.

Recommended:

* A multimeter (a cheap one is fine)

* A large capacitor (1000 μF, 6.3V or higher)

Since it's important for all the hardware to work together, let's talk in more detail about some of it so you know that you're ordering the right parts.

Power Supplies

Light strings take a lot of power—more than they can draw from the Pi. A Raspberry Pi's GPIO pins are rated for 16 milliamps per pin, or 50 mA across the whole GPIO header. A single NeoPixel or DotStar (just one pixel, not a string of them) draws 60 mA at full brightness. You could fry your Pi's GPIO if you tried to power multiple pixels that way.

You could tap into the 5-volt power supply you're using to power your Pi if it's a 2-amp or better supply *and* if you're not powering more than about 15 lights. But tapping into a USB cable is a pain; it's easier to use a separate supply, at least while you're testing. I like the cheap adjustable "wall warts."

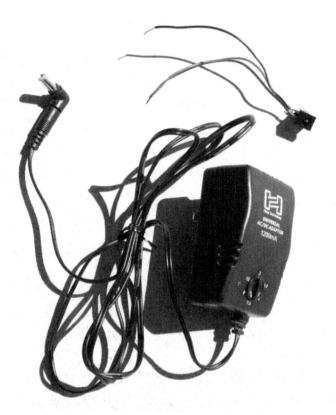

FIGURE 4.2: Adjustable "wall wart" power supply, along with a matching jack with bare wire leads to plug into a breadboard

They typically come with a selection of plugs, and you can either turn a dial or change plugs to get different voltages and polarities. You'll also need a jack that matches one of the plugs on the wall wart and can connect to your breadboard (bare wires) or directly to your light string.

Both NeoPixels and DotStars are nominally powered at 5 volts, though less is fine. Don't exceed 5 volts: they're reportedly very sensitive to over-voltage and you might damage your light string. If you can set your power supply to around 4.5 volts, that's perfect, but anything from 3.5 to 5 should work as long as it provides enough current to power your light string (60 mA times the number of lights). Use a voltmeter to make sure the power supply is producing what it claims—though the voltage may drop quite a bit once you add a load like a light string. A voltmeter can also ensure you don't have power and ground reversed.

Also, if you want to very safe about your light strings, connect a large capacitor (1000 µF, 6.3V or higher) between the power and ground terminals to protect against any voltage spikes your power supply might generate.

I'll address batteries and battery plugs at the end of this chapter.

DOTSTARS

APA102C light strings, also called DotStars, use a protocol called "two-wire SPI" to let your Raspberry Pi set color and brightness for every LED in the string. SPI stands for Serial Peripheral Interface bus; two-wire means, in this case, that you have one wire for data and a second wire for a "clock" signal to tell the light string when new data is available. That's a good thing: it's easy to drive the light string from a Raspberry Pi, much easier than with the older one-wire NeoPixel strings.

Of course, all electronic devices also have a power and ground wire as well. Connect the ground wire to the ground on your Pi, but remember, don't power the light string from the Pi's GPIO pins. Use a separate 3- to 5-volt power supply for the DotStar's power line.

DotStar strings have a direction: you need to attach your signal wires at the input end of the string, not the output end. If you look closely, the string probably has arrows indicating direction, from input to output. There may already be wires attached at one end or the other, but don't be fooled—some strings come with wires attached at the wrong end, in which case you should ignore them and solder your own wires to the input end. (If your string comes with wires at the output end, you can keep them in case you want to add a second DotStar string, or you can just cut them off.)

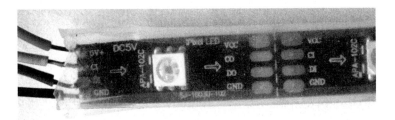

FIGURE 4.3: The arrows show the direction of the DotStar string.

If you're powering your DotStar at 3 to 4 volts, there's an easy way to wire it (Figure 4.4): connect your power supply's positive wire to the light string's +5V connection. Connect both grounds, from the Pi and the light string, to ground on your power supply.

Then connect Data Input (it might be labeled DI) to GPIO 10. If you're using a GPIO breadboard extension, GPIO 10 might be labeled MOSI, for "Master Out, Slave In." Your Pi is the master, and it's sending data out through MOSI to the slave, the light string. Connect the clock input wire (CI) to GPIO 11, also called SCLK. This wiring should work as long as the DotStar's input voltage is similar to the Pi's 3.3 volts. It might not work at 5 volts.

To test it, you'll need to download some software. Using a prewritten library is easiest so you don't have to handle all the details of SPI. In this case, the best supported library is provided by Adafruit. It's hosted on GitHub, and you can use git to download it. Bring up a terminal on your Pi.

If you're running headless, you may not have git yet. Type this command to be sure:

```
sudo apt-get install git
```

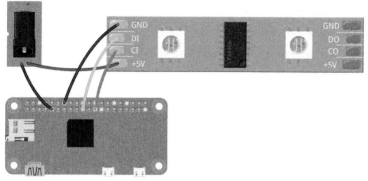

FIGURE 4.4: The simplest wiring for a DotStar string

Then download and install the DotStar library, with three more commands:

```
git clone https://github.com/adafruit/Adafruit_DotStar_Pi.git
cd Adafruit_DotStar_Pi
sudo python setup.py install
```

Time to test it! Edit the file strandtest.py with nano, Leafpad, or whatever text editor you prefer. Look near the beginning of the file for the line where numpixels is set.

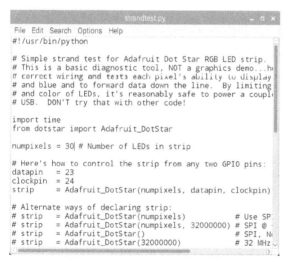

FIGURE 4.5: Edit strandtest.py and look for numpixels.

Change `numpixels` to the number of pixels in your string. A few lines down from that, look for the line that says

```
strip     = Adafruit_DotStar(numpixels, datapin, clockpin)
```

(the first `strip` = line, the one that's not commented out), and change it to

```
strip = Adafruit_DotStar(numpixels, 12000000)
```

That's 12 followed by six zeros. Save the file, then run

```
sudo python strandtest.py
```

With any luck, you'll see beautiful bars of color pulsing down your strip.

> **NOTE** SPI programs generally have to run with root permission, which is what `sudo` does for you. That means you should run light string programs from the terminal with `sudo`, even if you've been using IDLE for your other Python programs.

FIGURE 4.6: DotStar, wired up and running. The chip on the breadboard is a 74LVC245 level shifter.

If the LEDs don't light up, especially if you're powering the light strip at close to 5 volts, you may need a level shifter.

Logic Level Shifters

The Raspberry Pi's GPIO signals are only 3.3 volts. Since the DotStar expects 5V, sometimes the Pi's signals may not be strong enough, and you might need to boost them.

A logic level shifter can take input at 3.3 volts and convert it to 5. You can buy passive level shifters, sold under names like "Bi-Directional Level Shifter," but unfortunately those boards aren't fast enough to handle this job. You need an active level shifter. These chips have a lot of confusing names, but the names often include terms like "line driver" or "bus transceiver," sometimes with "3-state" or "tri-state" thrown in. The two most popular level shifting chips known to work with addressable LED strings are the 74LVC245 and the 74AHCT125. Figures 4.7 and 4.8 show wiring diagrams.

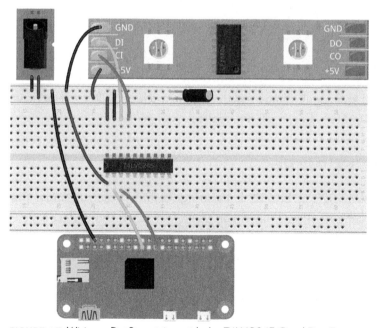

FIGURE 4.7: Wiring a DotStar string with the 74LVC245 Octal Bus Transceiver with 3-State Outputs

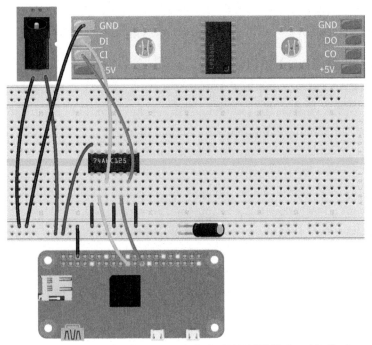

Wiring a DotStar string with the 74AHCT125 Quad Buffer/ Line Driver, 3-State

Once the wiring is ready, run sudo python strandtest.py again. If low signal voltage was the problem, a level shifter will get your DotStars glowing. If not, recheck your wiring.

NEOPIXELS

WS2812B or SK6812 light strings, sold by Adafruit under the name NeoPixels, have been around for years. They're less expensive than DotStars, and you can get them in all sorts of configurations: strings, jewels, circles, sticks, matrices, and individual pixels.

Unfortunately, they're a lot trickier to use with a Pi. Why? They need precise timing. They only have a data line, whereas DotStars have a data line and a clock line. Since there's no clock, the controller expects to get its data in a prompt, orderly fashion. That's easy with a microcontroller like an Arduino, but it's more difficult from a computer running Linux. A real operating system might be busy with other things just at the time when a signal needs to be sent to the light controller.

NeoPixels are also a little pickier than DotStars about input voltage. They have the same overvoltage problems as DotStars (try not to exceed 5 volts), but unlike DotStars, if you go too low, below 4 volts, you may see strange behavior.

The Simplest Hookup

As with DotStars, there's a simple hookup that might work if you're running around 4 volts to your light string. First, run power and ground from your power source to the light string. You'll also need a connection from the power source's ground to one of the Pi's ground pins.

> **WARNING** Be careful not to connect the external power source's positive terminal to any of the Pi's pins! You could burn out your Pi.

For signaling, run a wire from the light string's Data In to GPIO 18 (pin 12). You'll be using PWM to talk to the light string, and PWM is only available on a few Raspberry Pi pins, including GPIO 18.

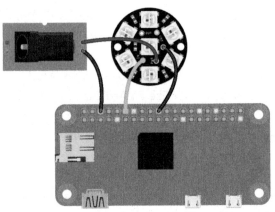

FIGURE 4.9: The simplest NeoPixel hookup. It may not work, depending on your voltage source.

The Software

For a long time, there was no way of driving NeoPixels directly from a Raspberry Pi. Then along came a library called rpi_ws281x. It even comes with Python bindings.

The library is written in the C language and uses a build system called *scons*, so you'll need to install some prerequisites to build it:

```
sudo apt-get install build-essential python-dev git scons swig
```

Once those are installed, build and install the library. At the prompt, type the following five commands:

```
git clone https://github.com/jgarff/rpi_ws281x.git
cd rpi_ws281x
scons
cd python
sudo python setup.py install
```

All that installation and building takes a little while, but once it's ready, you can change into the examples directory, where the Python example scripts are (in Linux, cd stands for "change directory"):

```
cd examples
ls
```

You should see the following:

```
SK6812_lowlevel.py    SK6812_white_test.py  multistrandtest.py
strandtest.py
SK6812_strandtest.py  lowlevel.py           neopixelclock.py
```

These are all example programs you can run. Start by editing strandtest.py in nano, Leafpad, or whatever text editor you prefer.

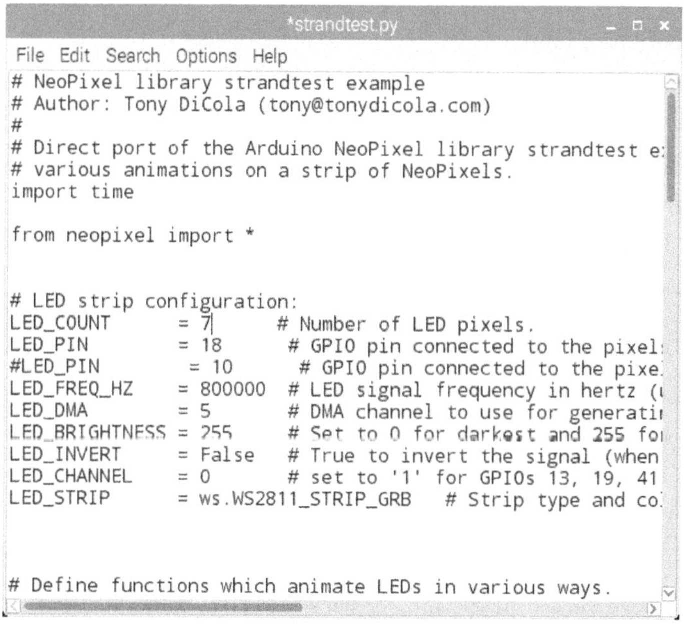

```
                          *strandtest.py             _ □ ✕
File  Edit  Search  Options  Help
# NeoPixel library strandtest example
# Author: Tony DiCola (tony@tonydicola.com)
#
# Direct port of the Arduino NeoPixel library strandtest e:
# various animations on a strip of NeoPixels.
import time

from neopixel import *


# LED strip configuration:
LED_COUNT      = 7|      # Number of LED pixels.
LED_PIN        = 18      # GPIO pin connected to the pixel:
#LED_PIN       = 10      # GPIO pin connected to the pixe.
LED_FREQ_HZ    = 800000  # LED signal frequency in hertz (
LED_DMA        = 5       # DMA channel to use for generatir
LED_BRIGHTNESS = 255     # Set to 0 for darkest and 255 fo
LED_INVERT     = False   # True to invert the signal (when
LED_CHANNEL    = 0       # set to '1' for GPIOs 13, 19, 41
LED_STRIP      = ws.WS2811_STRIP_GRB   # Strip type and co.


# Define functions which animate LEDs in various ways.
```

FIGURE 4.10: Editing strandtest.py

Change LED_COUNT to the number of LEDs you have in your string. Notice that LED_PIN is also set; if you want to fiddle with different pins later, you can do so here (but stick with 18 for now).

Save the file. Then, back in the shell, type

```
sudo python strandtest.py
```

(you have to use sudo because PWM, like SPI, requires root per-mission) and cross your fingers. If all goes well, you'll see a beau-tiful light show.

Troubleshooting

What if you don't see anything, or you see a few lights turn on but no light show? There are several things that could go wrong. These light strings are finicky.

Check your voltage level with a voltmeter and make sure it's around 4.5–5 volts and the right polarity (you don't have V+ and ground mixed up).

If voltage is good, it's possible the Pi's audio hardware is interfering—it uses some of the same PWM resources the light string needs. You can disable it. First, create a file named **/etc /modprobe.d/snd-blacklist.conf**. You'll need sudo permission to edit that file. Try this:

```
sudo leafpad /etc/modprobe.d/snd-blacklist.conf
```

(or nano instead of leafpad if you're running headless). Add this line:

```
blacklist snd_bcm2835
```

Then reboot.

> **NOTE** If you use your Pi to play music or other sounds, remove the snd-blacklist.com file when you're done with your NeoPixels. You can't do both at the same time.

For more information on this and other things that can go wrong, see the GitHub page for the library: *https://github.com/ jgarff/rpi_ws281x*.

The next likely culprit is logic levels—that pesky requirement that the WS2812B wants 5 volts and the Pi only provides 3.3.

To get around that, you might need a logic level shifter. For background on them, see "Logic Level Shifters" earlier.

Figures 4.11 and 4.12 show wiring diagrams for NeoPixels with the two most popular level-shifting chips.

With any luck, if your light string wasn't working before, a level shifter will get you going.

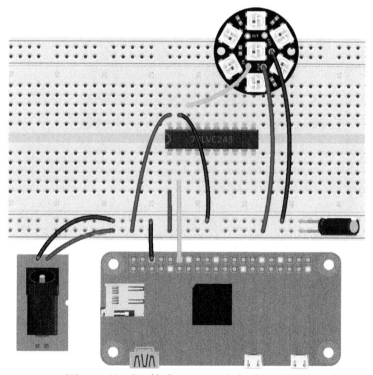

FIGURE 4.11: Wiring a NeoPixel light string with the 74LVC245 Octal Bus Transceiver with 3-State Outputs

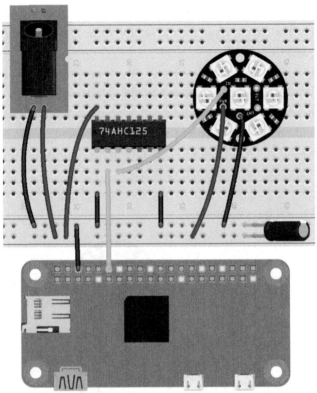

FIGURE 4.12: Wiring a NeoPixel light string with the 74AHCT125 Quad Buffer/Line Driver, 3-state

One last comment about NeoPixels. It's theoretically possible to drive them using one-wire SPI, similar to the two-wire SPI the DotStars use, rather than PWM. For SPI, use the Pi's GPIO 10, labeled "MOSI," rather than GPIO 18, and change the pin specified in strandtest.py. On the face of it, SPI sounds like it ought to be a more reliable method, but in practice, I've had no luck using SPI with NeoPixels. Feel free to try it, and drop me a line if you get it to work.

SEARCHING FOR TWITTER KEYWORDS

I know that it's tempting just to run strandtest.py forever. Ooh, shiny! But why not make the LEDs show something useful instead?

How about monitoring keywords on your Twitter stream so you can see trends visually with changing colors? (If you skipped the Twitter discussion in Chapter 3, "A Temperature Notifier and Fan Control," don't despair; skim this section, then skip ahead to "Web Scraping in Python" *for a non-Twitter option.*)

If you're still in the NeoPixel or DotStar library after running strandtest.py, get out of it: cd with no other arguments will get you back to your home directory. Create a file called **twit.py** that includes your Twitter code (import twitter and the init_twitter() function) from Chapter 3.

In Python-Twitter, GetHomeTimeline() will get your timeline—the list of recent tweets from everyone you follow. You can make a loop that checks your timeline every couple of minutes and prints any new tweet you haven't seen before. To try that, add this section to twit.py:

```
import time

if __name__ == '__main__':
    twitapi = init_twitter()

    tweets_seen = set()    # The set of tweets already seen

    while True:
        timeline = twitapi.GetHomeTimeline()
        print("\n===========================")
        for tweet in timeline:
            if tweet.id in tweets_seen:
                continue

            print("\n=== %s (%s) ===" % (tweet.user.screen_name,
                                         tweet.user.name))
            print(tweet.text)
```

```
        print("      %s" % tweet.created_at)
        tweets_seen.add(tweet.id)
    time.sleep(120)      # Wait two minutes
```

`GetHomeTimeline()` returns a list, and each tweet in the list is a `twitter.Status` object. The online documentation for Python-Twitter isn't very complete, but the library has built-in help you can get in the Python console or in IDLE:

```
>>> import twitter
>>> help(twitter.Api.GetHomeTimeline)
```

If you try that, it will tell you that `GetHomeTimeline` returns a sequence of `twitter.Status` instances, one for each message. Then you can find out what a `Status` includes:

```
>>> help(twitter.Status)
```

The important part of a `twitter.Status` is `.text`: that's the content of the tweet, so you can print `tweet.text`, and `tweet.text` is where you should look for keywords.

In the listing, `tweets_seen` is a set of all the tweets you've already seen, so you can check whether you've seen each tweet before and print it only the first time.

String Searches and Python Dictionaries

Once you have the text of a tweet, Python makes string searches super easy. For example, if you want to know whether a Twitter status includes "raspberry pi," you can use this:

```
if "raspberry pi" in tweet.text.lower():
    print "Another Raspberry Pi tweet!"
```

The `.lower()` function converts the status text to all lowercase, so you can search for "raspberry pi" without needing to worry whether it might be "Raspberry Pi" or "RASPBERRY PI."

Pick a few topics you want to match and keywords that tell you somebody's tweeting about each topic. For instance, I follow a lot of science and tech people. I also follow people who tweet about nature and the outdoors. How many tweets are related to Raspberry Pi or open source, compared to the ones about nature? You could set up a Python *dictionary* like this:

```
topicwords = {
    'tech':    [ 'raspberry pi', 'linux', 'maker', 'open source'],
    'nature': [ 'bike', 'hike', 'bird', 'bear', 'trail' ]
    }
```

A Python dictionary lets you index by keywords. `topicwords` is the dictionary. `topicwords['tech']` gets you the list of techie words. `topicwords['tech'][2]` gets you the third word in that list, or `maker[2]` (2 gives you the third word in the list, and not the second, because Python, like most computer languages, starts lists with 0).

You could use any categories, such as emotion words like "happy," "smile," "rofl," "sad," or "angry"; sports terms; terms related to politics; and so forth, depending on what you see in your Twitter stream. Adjust the list for your own preferences and experiment. You can use a lot more keywords than this example, though I recommend sticking to only two or three topics initially. Note that all the terms are lowercase, even those that are usually capitalized, like "ROFL"; that's because we're converting everything to lowercase before comparing the strings.

Now you can get your home timeline. Look through all the `Status.texts` and see if any of the keywords are there. To do that, loop over the statuses; then for each status, loop over the topics (tech and nature); then for each topic, loop over the keywords in that topic and see if that keyword is in that `Status.text`. Put this in your `twit.py` script, after the end of `init_twitter()` and before `if __name__ == '__main__'`::

```
def match_keywords(twitapi, topicwords):
    timeline = twitapi.GetHomeTimeline(50)
```

```
    matches = {}     # Build up a new dictionary of matches to return

for tweet in timeline:
    text = tweet.text.lower()
    for topic in topicwords:
        for word in topicwords[topic]:
            if word in text:            # Got a match! Add it.
                if topic in matches:    # saw this topic already
                    matches[topic] += 1
                else:            # first time we've seen this topic
                    matches[topic] = 1
return matches
```

match_keywords returns a new dictionary that looks something like this: { 'nature': 3, 'tech': 6. This indicates that there were three tweets with nature keywords and six that were techie. You can test it by printing its output from if __name__ == '__main__':.

```
    print(match_keywords(twitapi, topicwords))
```

Displaying Twitter Information on a Light String

You have the new dictionary returned from match_keywords. How do you show it on a light string?

How about showing a pixel for each tweet that matches a keyword, with a different color for each topic? The colors can cycle across the string or around the circle so it won't be boring to look at.

In the same directory where you have twit.py, edit a new file called twitterlights.py and make the first line import twit so it can use the Twitter code you already wrote. Add import time so you can sleep between updates.

Then include the module for whichever light string you're using, and set up the values it needs. Fortunately, Adafruit wrote their NeoPixel and DotStar libraries to have similar calls: they both have a Color type, and they both have strip.begin(), `strip.setPixelColor(i, Color(*color))`, and `strip.show()`. So after you initialize the light string, you can use the same code to control it whether it's a DotStar or a NeoPixel.

To initialize the string, you'll need the basic definition of the light strip, plus a way to define colors. So import `Color` as well as the strip itself (for NeoPixels, you'll also need to import `ws`), define your number of pixels as `num_pixels`, and initialize your strip. You can copy and paste from whatever worked in `strandtest.py`:

```
import twit
import time

# For DotStars:
from dotstar import Adafruit_DotStar, Color
num_pixels = 30
strip = Adafruit_DotStar(num_pixels, 12000000)
strip.begin()
```

   or

```
import twit
import time

# For NeoPixels:
from neopixel import Adafruit_NeoPixel, Color, ws

# LED strip configuration:
LED_PIN        = 18      # GPIO pin (18 uses PWM!).
LED_FREQ_HZ    = 800000  # LED signal frequency (usually 800khz)
LED_DMA        = 5       # DMA channel to use (try 5)
LED_BRIGHTNESS = 256     # 0 for darkest, 255 for brightest
LED_INVERT     = False   # True to invert the signal
LED_CHANNEL    = 0       # set to '1' for GPIOs 13, 19, 41, 45 or 53
LED_STRIP      = ws.WS2811_STRIP_GRB   # Strip type, color ordering

num_pixels = 7

strip = Adafruit_NeoPixel(num_pixels, LED_PIN,
                    LED_FREQ_HZ, LED_DMA, LED_INVERT,
                    LED_BRIGHTNESS, LED_CHANNEL, LED_STRIP)
strip.begin()
```

That takes care of initializing the light string. Now how do you use it to show the Twitter keywords?

Let's specify a color for each topic. Colors are specified as a list of (Red, Green, Blue), with each primary color going from 0 to 255. (0, 0, 0) is black (all colors off), (255, 255, 255) is white at full brightness (all three colors on), (255, 0, 0) is bright red, (0, 32, 0) is dim green, and so on. To show tech as purple and nature as green:

```
topiccolors = {
    'nature': Color(  0, 255,   0),
    'tech':   Color(255,   0, 255),
    }
```

The following code will display as many pixels of each color as there are tweets seen. If you see seven nature tweets and five tech tweets, it'll show seven green pixels and five purple pixels, advancing down the light strip or around the circle.

```
TWITTER_CHECK_TIME = 120       # How often to check Twitter
TIME_BETWEEN_PIXELS = .02      # Seconds from one pixel to the next
led_number = 0                 # Which LED are we setting right now?
tot_time = TWITTER_CHECK_TIME  # So we'll check immediately

twitapi = init_twitter()

while True:
    if tot_time >= TWITTER_CHECK_TIME:
        keywords_found = twit.match_keywords(twitapi, topicwords)
        tot_time = 0
        print(keywords_found)

    # Loop over the topics:
    for topic in keywords_found:
        # keywords_found[topic] is the number of keywords
        # we matched on Twitter. Show that number of pixels.
        # The color for this topic is topiccolors[topic].
        for i in range(keywords_found[topic]):
            strip.setPixelColor(led_number, topiccolors[topic])
            strip.show()
```

```
        led_number = (led_number + 1) % num_pixels
        time.sleep(TIME_BETWEEN_PIXELS)
        tot_time += TIME_BETWEEN_PIXELS
```

That looks good most of the time, but there's one more tweak to make it look even better. If the total number of Twitter hits over all the topics divides evenly into the number of pixels, or vice versa—suppose you have 20 pixels, and you saw seven tech tweets and three nature tweets, for a total of ten—then the colors will just stay in the same place rather than advancing around the string, and the display will look static. You can guard against that by taking the sum of the keywords found for each topic and using the modulo operator (%) to check for divisions with no remainder, and then adding a blank pixel in that case. Put this code right after `print(keywords_found)`, indented only four spaces, not eight:

```
    tot_hits = sum(keywords_found[i] for i in keywords_found)
    if num_pixels % tot_hits == 0 or tot_hits % num_pixels == 0:
        keywords_found['blank'] = 1
```

Whew! Lots of steps, but the result is pretty. Once it's working, try adding more topics in different colors.

WEB SCRAPING IN PYTHON

Don't care for Twitter, or just more interested in following some other website? No problem—you can write a web scraper.

"Scraping" means downloading a web page and searching through the text. Here's a very simple Python web scraper that accepts the same list of topic words as in the Twitter example and returns the same dictionary of matches:

```
import requests

def match_keywords(url, topicwords):
    r = requests.get(url)
```

```
    matches = {}

    for line in r.text.splitlines():
        line = line.lower()         # convert it to lowercase
        for topic in topicwords:
            for word in topicwords[topic]:
                if word in line:
                    # Add it to matches
                    if topic in matches:
                        matches[topic] += 1
                    else:
                        matches[topic] = 1
    return matches
```

This code splits the output into lines and counts the number of lines where there was a keyword match. You can test it with this:

```
if __name__ == '__main__':
    topicwords = {
        # Set up your topic words here, as in the Twitter section
        }

    print(match_keywords('http://WEBSITE_TO_SCRAPE', topicwords))
```

Of course, replace WEBSITE_TO_SCRAPE with whatever website you want to try.

This scraper isn't ideal, though, because 90 percent of a typical web page consists of menus, sidebars, ads, and JavaScript, and you don't want to scrape that. You only want to look at the text you'd see if you viewed the page in a browser. For that, you need to parse the web page's source, which you can do with a Python module called *BeautifulSoup*. First you have to install it (this covers both Python 2 and Python 3):

```
sudo apt-get install python-bs4 python-lxml python3-bs4
```

Then you can parse the web page and remove all that JavaScript. (Removing menus and sidebars is harder and is left as an exercise for the reader.) You can search for `<script>` tags, remove ("extract") them from the page, get only the text part of what's left, convert it to lowercase, split it into lines, and then run your keyword search. The `if __name__ == '__main__':` part doesn't change.

```python
import requests
from bs4 import BeautifulSoup

def match_keywords(url, topicwords):
    r = requests.get(url)
    soup = BeautifulSoup(r.text, "lxml")

    # Remove javascript:
    for script in soup(["script"]):
        script.extract()       # Remove all <script> tags

    matches = {}

    for line in soup.text.lower().splitlines():
        for topic in topicwords:
            for word in topicwords[topic]:
                if word in line:
                    if topic in matches:

                        matches[topic] += 1
                    else:
                        matches[topic] = 1
    return matches
```

You can get as fancy as you want to with BeautifulSoup and look only for certain tags, only for headlines, and so forth. When you're happy with your scraper, you can import it into a light string program, just as you would have with twit.py, except that you'll import scrape rather than twit, and instead of initializing the Twitter API, you'll call scrape.match_keywords('THE-WEBSITE-TO-SCRAPE', topicwords.

NOTE   The legality of web scraping still isn't a settled issue in most countries. There have been lawsuits in cases where a company scraped a competitor's website for commercial gain, but generally no one cares about individual scraping that isn't posted anywhere public. And of course, no one objects to Google scraping their websites to index them. When you're scraping websites, be nice and don't flood the site's connection; make sure your program sleeps a reasonable amount of time (a few minutes) between fetches.

MAKING IT PORTABLE: BATTERIES

Once you have your light string working, wouldn't it be nice to get it off your desk and make it wearable?

Since you'll be running the Pi as well as the light string off batteries, calculate the amps you expect your lights will draw: about 60 mA at full brightness times the number of pixels. Then add about an amp for the Pi, though you can probably get by with as little as 0.2 amps if it's idling most of the time, or a little more if it's going to be doing heavy computation. Batteries are rated by "amp hours," so if you can estimate the amps your project needs, you can make a first guess as to how long any given battery will run it.

One easy option is a portable USB charger with a lithium-ion battery.

These are sold as emergency chargers for cellphones, but they can power any device that expects to be plugged into a USB port. Typically they come with a USB A jack, so you can plug in a normal USB A to MicroUSB cable to get power to your Pi.

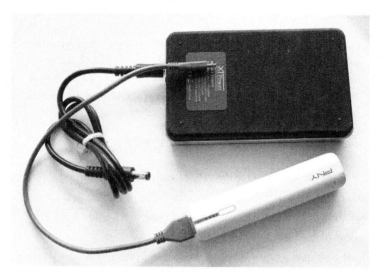

FIGURE 4.13: A couple of portable USB chargers

To power a light string in addition to a Pi, you'll probably have to make a Y connector that goes from the battery's USB plug to the light string. Even if you use separate batteries for the Pi and the light string, you'll still need a Y connector to link the two batteries' grounds together. Be sure to check the current output limitations (amps) on any battery you buy; small batteries may not have enough juice to power a Pi or a light string, let alone both.

You can use AA or AAA battery packs, but I don't recommend it. Three AA alkaline batteries provide 4.5 volts, and four nickel-metal hydride (NiMH) rechargeables provide 4.8. Either of those is within the acceptable voltage range, but the batteries won't last very long, and when they get tired the voltage will fall off steeply, to the point where your Pi might start behaving erratically.

Another option is lithium-polymer batteries, sold in hobby shops for powering radio control airplanes and cars.

> **WARNING** Lithium-polymer batteries require a special charger and are finicky about how they're charged. If you over-charge them or accidentally short them, they can easily start a fire. Lots of model airplane geeks use and love li-po batteries, but read up on them before committing.

A lot of NeoPixel tutorials recommend a single-cell li-po, which delivers 3.7 volts, a nice safe voltage for the light strings. But that's not enough voltage to power the Pi, so you'll need a separate battery or a step-up power converter.

If you use a two-cell li-po, available in hobby shops that sell model airplane supplies, you get 7.4 volts—far too high for either the Pi or the light string—but you can use a voltage regulator or step-down power converter to bring the voltage down to 5 volts. A voltage regulator might need a heat sink, so read up on the details of the regulator you choose. Step-down power converters are more efficient and might not need a heat sink. Either way, make sure it can handle several amps.

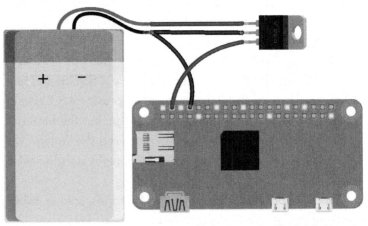

FIGURE 4.14: 5V voltage regulator used with a battery of higher voltage

Plugs for Portable Projects

No matter what battery you use, you'll most likely have to solder a cable with connectors. If you use one battery to power both the Pi and the light string, you'll need a Y connector that has power and ground from the battery going both to the Pi and to the light string. Even if you use two batteries with separate connectors, you'll still need some form of Y to connect the Pi's ground to the light string. Just like people, electronic gizmos need common ground to communicate.

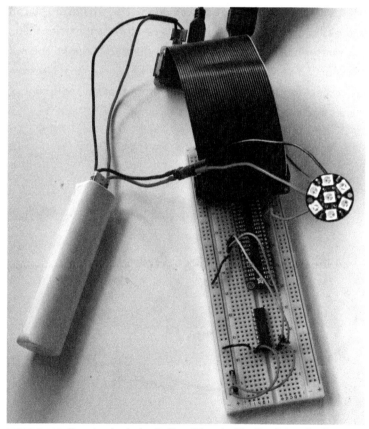

FIGURE 4.15: Running both the Pi Zero W and a NeoPixel Jewel off a USB backup battery, with a MicroSD plug (made from a spare USB OTG adapter) for the Pi and a mini-Deans connector for the NeoPixel

On the Pi's side, it's best to use a MicroUSB plug for power. You can provide 5V input power via GPIO pin 2 (the one labeled 5v), but there's no protection against voltage spikes as there is on the Pi's normal MicroUSB *Power In* jack. If you bought a pack of USB OTG adapters to get your USB hub working (Chapter 1), they also make nice solderable MicroUSB connectors.

For the light string (and the battery, if you're not using one that comes with a connector), you have your choice. There are lots of options: various types of connectors, Deans and mini-Deans, phone plugs (meant for audio), car and motorcycle plugs... the list is endless, and there's no standard. Use whatever you can find easily, especially if you have a local store that carries them. (No matter how many connectors you think you bought, you will run short on a Friday night when you're working on that last-minute project for the weekend.) Hobby shops that sell radio control planes and cars are good hunting grounds.

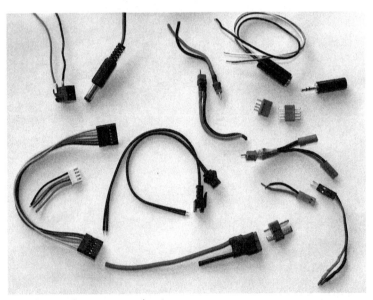

FIGURE 4.16: Connectors galore!

Whatever connectors you decide to use, get several of them, both male and female, so you can make adapters for several batteries, adapters from your wall wart to your wearable device, and so on.

There you have it: a wearable device that is not only pretty, but actually shows you useful information, updated in real time.

And that's it! Now you've built a selection of projects using the Raspberry Pi Zero W. You can use these projects as a basis for further adventures with the Pi. Don't forget to check out the GitHub repo, *https://github.com/akkana/pi-zero-w-book*, where you'll find all the code in the book (so you don't have to type it in yourself), wiring diagrams, and maybe a few additional examples of what the Pi Zero W can do.

Have fun!

INDEX